THE BILLION DOLLAR REPO MAN

My life as a Husband, Father and Luxury Asset Recovery Specialist

By Ken Cage

TABLE OF CONTENTS

INTRODUCTION – *All In*

Everyone has a dream of striking out on their own, taking that chance and making it big. The dream is to become incredibly wealthy and live in an enormous house with beautiful cars, big boats and fancy airplanes. I knew years ago I wanted to work for myself. It is who I am. I never dreamed I would be the one taking away peoples' big boats and fancy airplanes though.

I bought my company with my long-time friend Bob Weeks in 2005. Back then, if you would have told me I would be on TV or writing a book someday, I would have laughed at you. There is no way. I am just a regular guy from Delaware County, or Delco as local call it, a county that borders Philadelphia. I am a dad. I am a husband. I am a coach. I go to work to provide for my family, just like everyone else. I am not a television personality or author. Heck, I was just happy working for myself.

Before I bought my company, I had already traveled quite a strange career path. I had slung hazardous waste, worked at a local bank, led a security department at a hospital in center city Philadelphia and was an International Cash Manager for JP Morgan Bank. The last job I had before I bought my business is really the one that best prepared me to make the leap into buying my own high-end repo company.

I worked for Chrysler Financial and was a supervisor in the high-risk collections department. I managed a team of 18 collectors all working on cases that were 46 or more days past due and in risk of being repossessed. The team also recommended accounts for repossession and followed up with the repo agents when assignments were sent out. In short, I was the bank working the cases and assigning the repos. I knew what the finance companies wanted and how they worked.

More importantly, I knew about debtors. I knew when they were telling us stories and when they were truly going through hard times. I learned when to push and when to console. I have always said that I learned to be compassionate with debtors because of this job and I feel that is something that separates my company, IRG, from the others.

I also learned that sitting in an office with 600 other people wasn't my idea of a stimulating work environment. Now don't misunderstand, I made a lot of friends there and still talk to many of them 12 years after I left and remember more. That doesn't change the fact that I was not built for that environment. The most difficult thing for me was telling the people who were struggling to pay their bills that I was going to have to take their car away. It broke my heart every time I heard an employee tell these debtors to remember to remove the car seat from their minivans. Think about that for a second. Without that car, these people couldn't go to work, or the supermarket for formula or get that baby to the doctor or daycare. As a father, I struggled with that daily. I felt like I was taking their whole lives away. Some people could distance themselves from that fact. I couldn't. It weighed on me.

So, I decided it might be time to do something else and started thinking about owning my own business. I had been running my own sports training company for a couple of years and got a taste for being an entrepreneur. I enjoyed working with kids and trying to help them enjoy more success doing something they loved. I brought in a couple of friends of mine who were Division 1 athletes and we made a go of it.

I knew I couldn't go all in on a start-up though. I had 4 kids and a wife depending on me. While I loved doing my own thing, I knew I needed a regular paycheck. A startup would not offer that to me. My only option was to buy an existing company. The minute I committed to this, I began to chase this dream with a vengeance. It felt like this was an important first step for me.

I started looking at websites and looking at as many companies as possible. I reviewed well over 100 companies while doing my research. Most of them had financials that allowed me to eliminate them quickly. The companies that made sense were out of my price range. It was then I called Bob and asked him if he ever thought about owning a company. He said the timing was perfect and he was in.

I was looking over the opportunities and presenting potential businesses to Bob for his approval. One of the first companies we looked at in-depth was a golf training center near us. We were very interested. They had an indoor facility and driving range for off-season training and an equipment shop. They also had an outdoor driving range a few minutes down the road. Bob is an avid golfer, so we gave it every chance, but we could tell it just wasn't poised for success. We passed on this business and kept looking.

I kept seeing this "Luxury Repossession Company" based in Florida, so passed it on to Bob. We were interested so we began to pursue it. It was passing all of our tests. The price was acceptable. The skills required were investigations and sales. I had the investigations experience and Bob had the sales. I also knew the finance side of repossessions well. This made a lot of sense. I ran it by my wife.

"Absolutely not." my wife said. "You'll get killed."

That was gone as quickly as it came. I began scouring over dozens of companies and none of them made sense. Whether it was the financials or jobs I wasn't interested in, I was not finding anything. A few weeks later, my wife and I had just gotten the kids to bed, cleaned the house and were watching some late-night TV. Out of nowhere, we see a guy trying to repossess an airplane. We both watched intently as the repo guy on the screen was able to get onto the airfield, spot the plane and get it in the air in about three minutes. My wife and I looked at each other. "That looks pretty easy." I said. She agreed and gave her approval. That is all I needed. The next day, Bob and I began the journey to buy a company we called International Recovery & Remarketing Group. All told, it took us about six months to go through the process. We owned our own company.

It was never a goal of mine to repossess private yachts and jets. As a matter of fact, I was like most people and did not even realize this was being done as a career. In all honesty, I didn't even know very much at all about boats or airplanes. That never fazed me in the least though. I always feel that you can learn the technical side of a business. It is FAR more important to have the necessary personality traits and broader knowledge and those were not an issue.

The personality trait that is most important to me is my competitiveness. I love to compete. Whether its hockey, baseball, basketball, coaching, cards…whatever…I love to compete. In this profession, the competition is me vs. the debtor. I am trying to get his asset from him and he is trying to keep it from me. Who will win? Well...I think you know that answer. At the end of the repo, that is what gives me the most satisfaction. The fact that I won.

I also knew investigations were a huge part of this job and that is something I love. I have a degree in Mathematics from Cabrini University. Math is all about solving problems using logic and a step by step process to solve them. Investigations are the same. I needed to be able to find a small detail and use the proper steps to come up with the right answer.   I was very comfortable with that.

Finally, they say most repo men are adrenaline junkies. While I never described myself in that way, I have always been up to try something new, walk on the line a bit and be adventurous. I was always trying to get into places I didn't belong, or taking on personas and trying to get away with them. I lived with a lot of foreigners in my dorm at Indiana

University of PA and would often copy their accents and go around town claiming I was from these places. I had people believing I was from Scotland and actual Scots were faking. I loved seeing how far I could push the envelope.

I went so far as to create an entire back story with my good friend Chris Hassett. We were able to convince people we were from the small (fictional) town of Shaughneytown outside of Dublin. We would go into bars and parties with our best accents, telling made up Irish stories. It usually ended up with us getting into parties, free drinks and great conversations. While that might not be a junkie, these were skills I needed for my new job. The ability to think fast and cover your tracks without people knowing what is happening.

I made a decision to take a huge financial risk when I bought this company. If things hadn't worked out, I would have hurt my family in a major way. I had four kids between the ages of 3 and 11 when I bought the business. As devoted as I am to my career, nothing even approaches my need to provide a good childhood and life for my kids. That is the reason I took this shot. Yes, it was a huge risk and I had to consider all possibilities, but I also want my kids to be able to be proud of their Dad. I wanted them to see the possibilities for them and not see a Dad who was afraid to take a chance and then regretted it. With that mindset, I was more comfortable with the risks.

And it isn't just my own kids. I coach almost every team my kids play on in each sport. It is difficult to balance my personal and professional lives, but it is critical to me. I have finished cases, hopped on a plane and flown home to coach or watch a game. The parents that saw me before I bought my business still saw me at practices and on the sidelines for games like before. The only difference is now I was often coming from some crazy situation I was in a few hours before. They don't know though, so I often kind of laugh to myself about the contradiction of it all.

In the 3rd season of *Airplane Repo* I brought a film crew to tape my baseball team and league. Some of the crew asked why I pushed so hard to be so involved. Well, when I was 14 years old, I was diagnosed with bone cancer and had to spend a lot of time in the Children's Hospital of Philadelphia. I saw a lot of things that no teenager should ever have to see. My illness was misdiagnosed and I healed pretty quickly, but many of those kids aren't nearly as lucky.

That taught me a lifelong lesson that I still carry with me to this day. It taught me that kids should be allowed to be kids. They should be allowed to be innocent and free spirited. They should be allowed to spend as much time outside as possible, enjoying the fresh air. And they should be supported and celebrated. That is why I coach. If I can make one kid feel good about themselves and their experience, I have done something.

I have never stopped coaching and working to balance everything and I won't. I have learned how to plan and make things work better as time has gone on. I have still missed far too much, but my wife and kids are the greatest people I have ever met and they are forgiving. I thank God for them and for that daily.

CHAPTER 1: *Under the Gun*

It was a beautiful, sunny Florida day in January and there I was, standing aboard a $200,000 yacht and feeling pretty good about what I had just done. I had spent the last three days investigating a man who, until a few minutes ago had been the legal owner of this nearly new 43 foot Hatteras. The debtor was 85 years old. I can't say exactly how he made his money, but based on my extensive research, I can say his age hadn't stopped him from engaging in some less than reputable business.

I had begun like I normally do on an investigation. I started in my office in Orlando. I pulled investigative reports, looked on the internet and made calls. This debtor was known, but people either didn't know where the boat was, or they just wouldn't tell me. I wasn't sure which one it was, but I assumed the latter.

I checked some local marinas and places where a boat might be. I was having no luck. I wasn't very familiar with Jacksonville at that time, so I spent a lot of time checking things I soon found out I didn't need to. I had spent a lot of time in the field, so I decided to go to his two home addresses. There was no answer at either place. I looked over the reports again and found an address for a business the debtor was associated with. I went there next.

"Never heard of him."

That was the answer I got from the stand-offish Cuban guy behind the counter when I asked about the debtor. He was one of those guys that smiled at you and tried to convince you he was a nice guy, but you could tell he wasn't. I pushed on a couple of his answers, but he held fast to them. I knew the Cuban guy wasn't telling the truth, but rather than make a scene in his store, I continued looking elsewhere.

I tried several other dead ends. I checked on addresses, P.O. Boxes, neighbors and possible business associates. I was getting nowhere. Either it was true that nobody knew of this guy or, more likely, they knew and had a reason for not talking. I believed it was the latter but didn't know if fear or friendship was the motivating factor. I finally decided to call Bob and ask him to do some research while I was in the car.

It was after dark now and I was hungry and tired. I had eaten something light in the late morning and hadn't stopped for anything since. Bob and I had several back and forth phone calls and we were not able to come up with any new leads. On what seemed like the 10th phone call, Bob off-handedly offered an address for a Latin man who was listed as a possible owner for the business I had been to earlier in the day. For some reason, this associate didn't show up on my report, so I was happy that Bob was able to grab this nugget for me. If I was filming the show, this would have been a "Yachtsee" moment.

It was a little after 11PM when I got to the given address. It was a large house with all glass in the front. I could see a figure walking around and the TV was on. I got a little closer and could tell this was the same guy. It was an especially dark night. One of those where you could walk into trees without seeing them, and I did. I could tell there were no boats in the front or side of the house, so I went around to the back of the house. It was only then I noticed a small channel of water in there. A few more steps and I saw it. My bounty. It appeared to be huge and it glistened in the moonlight. I was excited.

It would have been incredibly foolish to try to start the boat, as the owner would have heard the motors. I decided the safest thing to do would be to order a towboat, but they told us the water levels were too low to pull the boat. After some attempted prodding on my part, I realized this would be a job we would run in the morning. The captain agreed to meet me at 6:45 am for a 7 am heist. It was back to the hotel for a few hours of sleep and then back to the boat.

This was one of the worst nights of sleep I can remember having on the job. I had left my house at 5 a.m. for a morning flight and it was now 12:30 a.m. the next day. I was beyond exhausted, but very much on edge. My mind was racing as I drifted in and out of sleep. What if the homeowner took the boat fishing in the morning? What if he saw me? What if he booby trapped the boat. I couldn't settle my mind as I attempted, unsuccessfully, to get some sleep. Every negative possibility entered into my head.

The next morning broke and I was up and ready quickly. I grabbed a coffee and muffin from the hotel buffet and out I went. The house was in a very quiet cul-de-sac in a neighborhood that looked as if everyone would notice a car that didn't belong. I decided to park at the end of the street and walk to the channel where I would meet the captain. It was a beautiful, warm sunny day. My wife and kids were stuck in a snowstorm in Philly, so I was feeling a bit smug about that, but it was on my mind. The captain was there right at 6:45 as planned and I hopped on the small tug which took me to the prize. The captain welcomed me with the news that water levels were high enough and we could proceed. It was on.

We quietly went down the channel behind 6 or 7 houses until we got to the Hatteras. The back of the house, like the front, was all glass. We knew we had to move quickly. This was a big case for us, with over

$20,000 commission on the line and I could feel the pressure of the case. More importantly, we were about to prove to the bank that hired us – and to my self – that we were ready to compete in the world of high-end repos. I could hear every wave splash against the boat and they sounded like claps of thunder. "Keep it quiet!" I excitedly whispered to the captain. He shot a daggered look back at me as if to sarcastically say "Oh, really?"

As luck would have it, the boat was turned the wrong way. This meant we would have to spin this big yacht in the tiny channel before we could get away from the house. Normally this would not be a major issue, but this was different. The longer we were behind the house and the more noise we made, the more likely we were to get caught. I had the worst thoughts running through my mind of what this guy would do if he caught me. Did he have weapons in the house? Would he use them in this quiet little neighborhood? The clock was ticking loudly in my head.

I hopped on the boat and I hurriedly tied the Hatteras to the tugboat who was ready to move. I knew the homeowner storing the boat could spot us at any time. I stayed low and kept scanning the yard. The last thing I needed now was a surprise and I was trying to avoid that at all costs. The captain said we were ready to go, so I laid on a cushion to stay out of site and off we went, spinning in a circle. I looked up into the beautiful, sunny sky and watched it spin pretty quickly. I kept thinking once we cleared the channel and got into the river, we would be safe.

Once we made the turn, I could still see the yard and the house. There was no movement in the yard and I couldn't see any lights going on inside. I was sweating and breathing heavy from the work and stress, but we were safe. I took a deep breath and called the repo into the local police. Calling the police is something we have to do on every repo to let them know what we are doing. We don't want a debtor calling in a stolen boat without the police being alerted to what really happened. A few minutes later I was about done with the call and the officer asked "Is everything ok there?" I informed her that everything was fine and we were away from the house. All good.

We were maybe 30 minutes onto the river and I was done taking pictures and checking out every inch of the boat. This was the fun part of the repo. We were puttering along behind to tow boat in a relaxed ride. I could sit on the deck and just enjoy the ride. The sun was beating on my face and I couldn't wait to tell this story. I knew it was a good one. I try to take a second to appreciate my situation, so I remember taking a deep breath of the ocean air before I shot a quick text to my wife. I always make sure I let her know I got the boat and am in a safe position. I then took a seat again to continue to enjoy my ride.

A minute or so later, I noticed another boat behind us in the distance and I saw its nose was up. "Whoever that is, they sure are in a rush to get somewhere." I thought. As it got closer, it occurred to me that the homeowner had a second boat behind his house and this trailing boat looked a lot like that one.

I tried to start the motors, but no luck. I knew there was no way we were going to outrun any boat hooked to a tug. Just then the captain began to realize what might be going on and he got scared quick. He asked if that was the other boat and at this point I knew it was. "Yeah, that's it." As the boat came more clearly into view, I could see what looked like the Cuban from the auto shop at the helm. It looked like he had the boat maxed out to its top speed, which seemed like 40 mph or more. I could also make out another person on the front of the boat. He was leaning forward on the railing and was pointing guns at us. We were know facing the worst-case scenario.

It quickly occurred to me that I had underestimated the element of danger in this line of work. I knew there was the potential for things going wrong on repossessions, but I had convinced myself...and my wife...that those things were saved for cars and trucks. Not the high-end repossessions. When I was completing my due diligence, I had found many cases of violence, injury and death on smaller repos, but not on a boat repo. How could I have miscalculated so badly? I felt fear in a way I had never felt it before. I had worked in a hazardous waste plant and watched 85-gallon drums explode, but this was far more frightening. My training in emergency services prepared me for times like these, however. I took a second to clear my mind and then started to make an action plan on how to survive.

The first decision I made was to call in a Mayday to the Coast Guard. The Coast Guard informed us they were on their way. Time was short though. The Cuban was catching us and fast. If he caught us, I knew he would use those guns. Nothing good could come from that. For a brief second, I knew the help wouldn't arrive in time. I thought about coaching my daughter's soccer team and shooting hoops with my boys. I thought about my wife. The sweat was pouring off of my hairline. I could feel my heart beating. The captain pushed the tug as hard as he could, but it wasn't helping much. Then, out of nowhere, we saw the rescue vessels. They were approaching like I had imagined the Calvary had.

Seconds later, the nose of the chase boat went down very quickly and the boat veered hard left to begin going in the other direction. The chaser became the chased as the rescue vessels went to confront the chaser. He tried to run, but it was just a matter of seconds until that chase ended.

We learned that the captain of the vessel had a warrant for his arrest. While the Coast Guard never tells you a lot, I found out from some other contacts that he was charged for drug and weapons charges. Turns out this guy was as bad, if not worse, than that original smile told me.

This case happened in 2006, just a few weeks after we bought the business. Since that time, I have done over 2,000 repos, but that was my baptism in this business. As I had just learned, there was a lot more to this job that I had anticipated. Luckily, it was too late to turn back now.

If you thought this was the end of the story, you would be incorrect. Two weeks later, the assignment came over to repossess the other boat. Since the guy keeping the boat could no longer protect it, the repo went easy. It was the perfect cherry to top off a pretty wild story though. Not only did we get the boat they were willing to go to jail to keep us from, we got the boat that they used to try and kill us. Yes, that is the way a repo story should end.

CHAPTER 2: *Repo Rookie*

There was a loud, long, sickening sound and I knew exactly what it was.

"Well that's it," I thought. "We're out of business."

After completing forty hours of training and acing the test, I became a licensed repo man in Florida. I learned all the laws and a few tricks – basically how you are "supposed" to do the job. Then I got to work.

A week or two after we bought the company, a bank sent us an order for a $300,000 58-foot Hatteras. I was very excited and quickly became laser focused on the job. This was my first involuntary surrender, meaning the first case where the owner wasn't just turning over the boat. I was going to have to find it and take it from them. This was a REAL repo. That's what this job is all about.

I began by doing some research in the office. Even as recently as 2006, the technology was lacking, to say the least. There was some information that could be found online, but not a ton. So, I did all of the online work I could do and then began placing calls to several people both within and outside of my network. I was only able to get some tidbits so I headed out on the road.

I went to Florida's Gulf coast to begin my search. All information I had said the boat was likely in this area. Florida is usually the state with the 2nd or 3rd highest boat ownerships in the country. Michigan and California are the other two states in the top 3 and they tend to fluctuate. What this means is, finding a boat in certain parts of the state are extremely difficult and where I was going was one of those areas. Even one as large as 58-foot can prove challenging. This was going to be like trying to find a needle in a haystack. I was new to the game though and I was full of energy. What I lacked in experience and more than made up for in passion.

I started by walking the marinas and dry storage areas. I walked mile upon mile trying to find a solid lead. The first thing I learned about my new career was that, no matter what you see on TV, repos don't generally come together very quickly. They take time. Judging by an episode of *Airplane Repo*, you would think I get the order and then stroll onto an airport or marina and magically discover the asset I am looking for. The part you never get to see is the days of walking and looking and calling just trying to get a lead.

After three days of looking I got what I considered a good lead. I noticed an old fisherman was chartering boats in the area. I struck up a conversation with him and, as luck would have it, he knew of the boat. He sent me to a place called Treasure Island and I began to look there. Word was it was for sale so I started checking as many brokerages as I could. I walked, drove and asked questions. I was getting closer. I could feel it.

I spent the entire day looking in the area and continued to hit dead ends. While I was somewhat frustrated, I kept reminding myself that these were not dead ends. They were just places I could scratch off of my list meaning I was narrowing down the places the boat could be. All I had to do was continue pushing forward and I would find my boat.

It was now pretty late on a Sunday night and I was starving. I wanted to stop to eat, but knew of a decent sized marina that had a brokerage with a less than sterling reputation that I had to check on first.

After that, I thought I would go to a nice seafood place I noticed on the drive. Hopefully it would be a celebration dinner.

It was a quiet night in December, so there weren't many people walking around when I pulled into the parking lot. As a matter of fact, it was dead. This was a relief to me. The fewer people that saw me poking around, the better chance I could get out of here without tipping anyone off. I began to walk the marina and got close to the broker's area when something immediately began to stand out. It was a massive white flybridge larger than anything I had seen on any boat I had been on. It drew me quickly to it in hopes it might be the one. As I got closer, I could make out the name on the back of the boat.

"That's it," I thought. Yes!! This was my boat! I had found it. What a rush! I pumped my fist in the air and took a second to savor this small victory. I knew that the tough part still was in front of me. The tough part was getting it out of the marina. I quickly surveyed the area and saw it was a fairly straight shot out of the marina into the bay. "This should be a simple one." I thought to myself.

At the time, I was still considered an "intern" by the state, so I needed to work with a licensed agent in order to do the repo legally. I called my contact and he told me he was busy and we would do it the next day. Not exactly what I wanted to hear. I always hated being hamstrung by another person's choices. Especially a person who had no financial stake in the repossession. But I was still feeling very good about what I had accomplished and went to that seafood restaurant for a good meal.

We met the next day and decided to wait until the brokerage closed the following night to get moving. The other repo guy decided to use his captain and tow company. He also insisted we hire yet another repo man for this job who was a local to that area. I hated the idea and thought it was overkill. Four repo guys for a pretty basic repo in Florida was excessive. It turned out the other guy wanted to spread the wealth with his friend and I didn't have a choice. This turned out to be a great learning experience for me.

When the time came to move on the boat, Bob and I went together. We discussed the repo on the way over to the restaurant where we were to meet the other repo guy. I told Bob I was uncomfortable with the strategy being used and thought we were using too many people. I was also concerned about the boat still being where I had found it the day before. I was anxious and uneasy, but we both attributed this to my excitement of doing this big repo.

It was about 6:45 p.m. when we finally decided to make the move. Bob and I were relieved when we saw the boat sitting in the same slip as the day before. I began to relax a bit and convinced myself that my anxiety was unfounded. We watched the boat for 15-20 minutes until knew there was no activity near the boat. It was now dark outside, so we all felt it was safe to go for it. The other guy gave us the que to jump on the boat and on that call, off we went. He was on the boat for about 30 seconds and then got off. Bob and I frantically untied the lines and began to push the boat off of the dock when we noticed the captain tying the boat to the tug on the bow.

Bob and I were so focused on our jobs, that we didn't notice the captain that had boarded the boat. When we first noticed him, were shocked. The captain could barely stand up straight. He was staggering from side to side and smelled horrible. This captain was stone drunk. To make matters worse, the tow boat was a 10-12 foot rowboat with a small motor and a guy driving that looked like he had spent the day in the same bar as our captain. We were in trouble here. These guys were not prepared to help at all and we were stuck with them.

We tried to think of an alternative plan as the boat was being pulled from side to side by the tiny tow boat. The captain saw the near panic in our faces and told us "Relax. As soon as I get the boat running we will get rid of the tow and go on our own." We were not reassured, to say the least. Instead of being towed by a tiny boat, we were going to be on board with a captain who was not exactly sober. We wondered how it could get worse. We were about to find out.

The captain couldn't get the boat started. For whatever reason, it just wouldn't crank. We assumed it was, at least in part, due to the operator's condition. This is a normal issue with the assets we repo. Generally, the bank payments are not all that is being skipped. The normal maintenance of the asset is often skipped as well. To make matters worse, the captain couldn't get the electric on in the boat. We had no running lights and no interior electricity at all. This was becoming a disaster.

It was now pitch black and we were still in the inlet trying to get to the open bay. After some unsuccessful attempts to get the boat cranked, the captain came up with a "great" idea. He told us to go down to the engine room with flashlights and screwdrivers. He told us to jam the screwdrivers into the sparkplugs to get the motors to crank. Desperate, we followed his instructions

I have led emergency teams in the past, so thought a briefing with Bob would be a good idea. There were two engine room doors and two engines, so I told him to go to the back door and work on that engine, while I worked the front side. Bob and I needed something to go right, so down we went with a plan. The flashlights were flickering which made it impossible to see. I was feeling my way down the steps and thought I was close to the engine room door.

Out of nowhere, I hear a THUD and feel a driving pain in my head. The unexpected jolt sent me back into a wall. I yelled out to see what it was. It turns out Bob slammed the front door open in his haste to check the engines and split my head open. That plan we came up with at the top of the steps was forgotten by the time we reached the bottom.

"What was that?" he asked

"My head!"

"Oh...are you bleeding?" he inquired

"I don't know because I can't see. But my hand is really wet so probably." I answered angrily.

"Oh" he said.

That's right. Just oh. No sorry. Nothing like that. Luckily, we were below deck because I really wanted to see him swimming with some gators about now. But we had a job to do. We raced upstairs with the news that his idea didn't work. Before we could get up the steps, we heard the most horrific SCREECHING from the front of the boat to the back.

"What is that?" I heard Bob yell.

At that point, I did not know exactly what the sound was. I just knew it was along the side of the boat we had just repossessed. It sounded as though something jagged was gashing the side of our boat.

The entire side. The sound began and just didn't want to end. I was certain that, not only was there a bad scratch, but there had to be additional damage as whatever was running up the side of our boat was digging a lot deeper than a scratch. I was trying to prepare for the worst.

It turned out to be a long night. Stopping wasn't an option. The other repo guy decided to store the boat behind a house which was about 35 miles away, so we would be towing this boat for several hours more in the dark. Normally being towed at night with no lights isn't close to ideal, there was a part of me that was relieved that we couldn't see the damage. "I guess that you don't have insurance we can call on about this, huh?" I asked the captain. As you might expect, he got belligerent and tried to explain how this wasn't his fault.

Finally, after about 9 hours of being towed, we finally docked the boat. It was about 4:30 am and Bob and I each found a salon to sleep for an hour or two before the sun came up. It wasn't actual sleep, as you might imagine. Just a few minutes to lay our heads down. When we got up, we knew we had to check to see how bad the damage was. We braced ourselves for the worst. We decided I would be the one to look first, so I leaned over the starboard side with squinting eyes. I was amazed with what I saw. "Oh no…Bob, come take a look." I told him. He was mildly panicked as he came running to look. Somehow, as loud and horrific as the sound was, there wasn't a scratch. Nothing. We couldn't even see where contact was made. We had gotten lucky. "Next time, watch the damn door." I told him as he complained about me fooling him.

That's how we were initiated into the repo business. I may have gotten my head sliced open, but more importantly we learned some valuable lessons that night. The old-school way of doing these repos meant using the buddy system. It meant watching a drunken tugboat driver tie a rope to the bow of your boat and smash it into things. It meant allowing a drunk captain to make decisions on how the boat would be transported. No more.

The best result of this case, aside from the commission for the sale, was the confidence I gained. I knew I had a better way to do this work than what I was being taught. From now on, we were going to make sure everything was done to the letter. We would hire certified and licensed tow boats, captains, pilots and maintenance people. There would be no more counting on luck. We would make this work OUR way. The right way.

Bob and I spent the next 12 hours taking inventory of all of the personal property on the yacht. We discussed what we wanted the "IRG way" to be. We discussed what our policies and procedures would be. This was the day that changed things for the better for our company. Never again was the theme.

We have since done thousands of repossessions. We have never used anyone who wasn't licensed, insured, bonded, sober and professional. We have never had an incident like that again. We have stuck to the plan of the early December morning and it has served us well.

CHAPTER 3: *The 54-Footer*

A week or two after the Hatteras repo, I decided to go to a banker's conference in Ft Lauderdale to see if I could drum up some business for this new venture. This was a pretty typical banker's conference. The attendees were mostly older guys who were happy to be out of the office and at a bar. There was some training, but none that applied to us.

I introduced myself to everyone I could and let them know I was the new guy with a background exactly like theirs. I received many polite thanks, handshakes and small talk but nothing more. Then a met a younger maritime attorney from Orange County, CA. He told me he was a former minor league baseball player and we hit it off quickly. We spent the night having a couple of drinks and talking baseball, mixed in with a bit of business.

He then shifted abruptly and looked at me

"Listen, I know you are new to this. Can you handle a tough case?" he asked.

"Of course I can. I would love to handle your toughest case." I quickly responded.

He stared me down a bit and, whether he believed me or not I don't know, but decided to give me a shot.

"We have been looking for this boat for nearly two years." He told me. "My client is pissed at me for not finding it yet. I am embarrassed. Find it and I will make sure you get more business."

With one hand shake I got a challenge and a promise. More importantly I was assigned what was, for now, my largest case to date. It was a 54-foot Sea Ray with an estimated value of $800,000. The boat was known to be in Ft Lauderdale when it was last seen two years before, but the vendor working on the case was local and very well-known, so we knew the boat couldn't be there. We also determined the owner was from New England and had a place in the Bahamas. We had some leads.

We began by spending a great deal of time in the office. We were trying to get a better idea of where this yacht could be. We learned of some connections the debtor had in Vero Beach, FL so we ran there and looked everywhere, but came up cold. We got a case in the Bahamas so ran the Abacos Islands, but found nothing. While on this trip, we did make a connection at a marina. He agreed to help us look through the other islands on a contingency basis. We then got a tip in Providence, Rhode Island, so I ran there to look. Again, we came up empty.

This went on for over five months. We were looking for this boat nonstop, high and low. We were working a bunch of contacts and casting as wide a net as possible. Every other case on the east coast and the islands, was extended a day or two to look for this boat. I probably walked fifty miles or more worth of docks by myself. It was some real old-school gumshoe stuff. But despite our best efforts, we were no closer to seizing the yacht.

When we are looking for an asset, we get investigative reports listing the debtor's relatives, friends, business associates and more. It is a huge, detailed report covering anything that might have even a remote bearing on the case. In this instance, the owner of the boat was in the construction business. He had done some work in South Florida during the winter months, but nothing concrete.

We also learned from the report, that he had done some work with a realtor in Ft Lauderdale. But this wasn't anything earth shattering. Based on our investigation, this was just another name and phone number. We put this in the file with the reports, newspaper articles, sales paperwork, brokers, contacts, phone numbers, titles and so much more. The file was literally 3 inches thick.

We were at the end of our rope and frustrated. We have a company policy that we do not bill for out of pocket expenses until a case is solved or closed and these expenses were building. I was really beginning to feel the pressure on this case. Now, to top it off, the client said if we didn't come up with something soon, he would pull the assignment and go another route. The stress was palpable.

I met with an investigator over lunch to discuss the case. This particular person may not have been a repossession specialist, but he knew how to investigate. I went over the places I had looked, the information I had and the contacts I had made. I did this pretty routinely as a sounding board of sorts, but also to see if he saw anything obvious I was missing. I did most of the talking as I recited all of the work I had done. He would ask me some questions and I would respond in great detail.

"Sounds like you checked everywhere but where it was last seen." He said.

"I know that. You have to understand our competitors have been working the case for 18 months. That is where they are. It is their own neighborhood. No way it could be there." I confidently answered.

"Why?" he asked.

"You have to be kidding me. There is no way." I responded.

"You really don't know for certain that they looked for the pen to fill out the folder, now do you?" he asked.

At that, I was challenged for an answer I didn't honestly have. I decided to head to Ft Lauderdale that weekend with Bob and start from scratch. We booked our flight for that Friday morning because an early spring blizzard was due in Philly and we needed to get there. We landed in Florida to 82 degrees and all sunshine. I took this as a positive omen.

Bob and I literally spent 15 hours each of the next three days driving, walking, talking and looking. Marinas, dry storage stacks, maintenance shops, brokerages and even a charity fundraiser. We did it all and called as many people as we could trying to get the one tip. We got some cold tips, but still nothing firm.

I sat in my hotel room Sunday night after the long days of driving throughout southern Florida and began taking notes of what we had done. I compiled what I had written with what I remembered to go over everything we had done. Most of what I had was not helpful, except to eliminate that marina or person from the investigation. The only thing of interest at all was the possible connection the debtor may have had with the realtor.

At breakfast the next morning, I told Bob we were going to check out the realtor's office first thing. It was in the middle of town, so I grabbed a coffee and off we went. I wasn't sure of the connection, but there was some reason this person kept coming up on his report, so they had worked together at some point. When we pulled up to her office, I noticed it was a plain, low-key office. This disappointed me. I was hoping for a fancy, high-end realtor who would be involved with the owner of a million-dollar boat.

I quietly knocked on the door and walked in. When I saw her, I introduced myself and asked if she could talk. I told her I was from up north and had a friend that was selling his boat. I told her I was interested in looking at it, but didn't have an address. I told her he had mentioned her to me before, so thought I would ask her if she knew where it was. It was a long shot, but it seemed to work with her.

"When did you last talk to him?" she asked.

I needed to answer quickly, without hesitation and be somewhat vague. "A week or so ago." I answered.

"I have been trying to reach him for a couple of weeks and he never returns my calls." She told me.

"I am having the same problem. That is why I came to see you. He hasn't answered my calls either. Maybe they are having bad weather up there." I said.

She bought it. She then proceeded to tell me where the boat was being kept the last time she saw it. She told me the debtor had a few lots on the water that he intended to build on and he ran out of cash. She told me the boat was docked behind one of the lots. "It has been there since the hurricanes of 2004." She said. She said she hadn't seen it in several months, but if it was still there, she wouldn't be surprised if there was some damage.

I casually small talked about it for a minute or two, trying not to blow my cover. I then thanked her and walked to the car. Bob was still in the car, so he parked it across the street in a convenience store parking lot. My heart was racing, but I couldn't let her know this. I slipped into the car as cool as I could.

"Got it." I told him.

We sped to the location she gave me. She had described the area perfectly. There were construction crews and cement trucks working on empty lots. All of the lots backed up to the water, which had old, beat up docks attached. There were no numbers, so I went up to ask one of the workers where the lot was I was looking for. He told me it was the end of the block. Again, trying to act as cool as possible, I strutted down the street. There was a construction project next door to our lot that was obstructing my view. I kept walking until I could see and sure enough, there was the boat. I had found it.

I sent Bob to the boat and had him board. At that, a foreman for the project on the adjacent lot approached. "Whats going on?" he asked. I responded with some small talk and began to talk about the house they were working on. He answered calmly, then asked why Bob had boarded the boat. I told him we had just bought it and we were moving it. "Son of a gun, Tony finally sold that thing." The foreman responded. I shook my head and he seemed genuinely happy at the thought. Since he seemed pleased, I started asking some questions about the boat. He confirmed that the boat had not been moved in 3 years or more. I shook my head and we small talked for a few minutes more. We shook hands and I left, with the foreman none the wiser.

I immediately went to the boat to see what we had. It was not in bad shape. Just needed some TLC. There were no bumpers on the boat and I could see where the boat had been damaged banging into the seawall for the last 2 years. I boarded the boat and asked Bob how it looked. He thought it looked very good and, considering how long it had been sitting he was right. The boat had not been started in years, so I was not going to attempt to take this away on its own bottom. I called the local towboat company and the waiting game was on. I untied all but one line just in case someone wanted to show up and start trouble. The clock was ticking and I was uptight. Bob fell asleep in the cabin. Luckily, there were no confrontations on this one.

The towboat pulled up and tied me up properly. After the Hatteras repo, this was a welcome sight. Off we went, with me on the bridge enjoying the weather. I decided to call my wife from here, giving her the good news. She was in an especially good mood because school was canceled due to the snow and, as a teacher, "snow day" is a cherished term. She was baking cookies with the kids at home, while I was enjoying a ride on a yacht in South Florida. It was a good day.

Then I finally got to do what I had been waiting to do since I got the assignment at the bankers conference. I got to call my client. It is the one thing I had been imagining doing every time things got a little bit difficult. I kept reminding myself it would all be worthwhile when I made the call. However, once I made the call I toned it down a lot from what I had imagined.

"Hey Ron. I got the boat." I confidently told him.

"You did? Where was it?" He asked.

When I told him where, he immediately shot off "That's less than a mile from the other guy's office."

"It's 3 blocks away to be exact." I told him.

He went off. Attorneys have to employ a mastery of the language like few other professions and my client was proving that, in truck driver talk.

Since my dad was a truck driver and he wasn't mad at me, I enjoyed the colorful way he spun the words together. He was furious that a company had supposedly been looking for this boat for two years when it was in their neighborhood the entire time. He kept asking me how to justify their performance. Each time I told him I couldn't. I later found out the same bank hired them for a boat they couldn't find for two years. They assigned it to someone else who found the boat in the marina next door to them. As you can imagine, this was a nice feather in our cap.

We were not an approved vendor for the bank, so we couldn't sell the boat on this case. As a result, we were not able to make all that much on this case. It was a monumental case for IRG though. We had concluded an attorney's toughest case. We were now a major player in the industry. The client did give us more cases. The bank that the attorney and I worked for, gave us 600 repos over the course of the next few years, so all in all very profitable.

I can't speculate as to how the other company could have missed that boat. It was literally sitting right under their noses. Maybe they didn't look as thoroughly as they should have. Maybe they just were not very good. Maybe they felt entitled to cases without putting the work in. It probably didn't mean as much to them as it did a couple of newcomers. To us, this case was huge.

This case also provided another vital learning experience. In this line of work, a tiny piece of information could be the piece that cracks the entire case wide open. One insignificant phone call, could be the one that lands you the boat. I looked at the realtor's name and address 5 times or more and never flinched. Never thought to look for more information. It wasn't until I did that the repo fell into place. That is how it always worked. You cannot assume anything. You never leave a stone unturned. And at the end of the day, you don't stop looking until you are sitting on the boat.

After this case, we became known as the ones who could find the difficult ones. Banks would come to us with their toughest ones at conferences and we would find them all. Your reputations means everything in this field and, after this case ours was gold.

CHAPTER 4: *The Snoopy Plane, The Tri-Pacer and More Repo Lessons Learned*

There were two big benefits to buying an established company, rather than starting our own. Having an established name, even with a less than sterling reputation, opened doors at some banks we wanted to work with. It also provided the potential for immediate income, which is critical when you are the father of four kids. In our case, the other major perk was Glenda.

Glenda came with the company. She had worked for the company prior to the purchase and she was committed to working with us. She was supposed to be the secretary, the role she had maintained previously. I had seen her handle tasks like order lunch, fix coffee and run errands while I was looking at the business. We assumed that was her role and Bob and I began thinking of ways to expand this. In all honesty, I don't need anyone ordering my lunch or fixing my coffee. I certainly wasn't interested in paying someone to do it for me.

When I began working with Glenda, I quickly noticed she was not being utilized properly. After about a month, I informed her that she was overqualified for the job she had. She looked at me confusedly and asked what I meant. I told her all that I saw she could do and didn't feel her talents were being utilized in any way. It was then that I gave her a promotion. Once this happened, she began to trust me a little bit more and I saw more of her personality. She has a fun, devious side to her that I enjoyed watching and listening to. It also made me very happy she was on our side.

I began to have her work some more cases with me and make some of the calls. It is a known fact that many people perceive women as more trustworthy, so I had her place some calls to try and locate assets we were looking for. I was amazed at how good she was. At one point, she worked nine cases and found the asset on the first call each time.

We had something really good going. We were both in the office, so could communicate easily. I would take the order from the fax machine, begin to do the investigative work and give her some possible locations and phone numbers. She would take this information, choose which place she thought our asset was and get a positive ID. I would then fly out of the office to secure the asset. It was all I could have hoped for.

Then one day, we got an order for an old Beagle airplane. The Beagle is a 1960's seven seat, twin engine airplane known for being used by the Royal Air Force. It was a unique and cool little airplane, but this made it much more likely that we would get exposed if we came with our normal routine. We had to try something different.

I got a lead that the airplane might be at a museum in the southwest. I had Glenda dial them up and explained to her my hesitations about getting caught. I advised her to be extremely discreet and she said she understood. It was then I met "Stacy".

"Hi darlin. I am calling to see if you have a Snoopy plane there." Glenda said in her best "dumb-blonde" voice.

I started waving my hands wildly and mouthing "It's not a SNOOPY plane...it's a BEAGLE"

But Glenda knew exactly what she was doing. She went back and forth with the nice woman on the other end, who was trying to figure out what "Stacy" was talking about. Finally I hear the woman say "Sweetheart, do you mean a Beagle?"

"Yes, that's it. I knew it had something to do with Snoopy." Glenda answered and giggled. And just like that, Glenda's new character, Stacy, had just found out where the airplane was. I had it recovered the next morning. This was an incredible revelation for me and the company.

As I was quickly learning, it doesn't matter how crazy your approach might be, as long as it is legal and it works. In training, they taught me some basic ways to get a repo accomplished. The problem is, I don't fit the bill of a "normal" repo man. I don't try to be a threatening person. I sound like a normal guy. I look like a banker. I couldn't use the conventional old-school tactics. I WOULDN'T. I had to learn to use what I have to my advantage. It didn't take long to discover how many advantages I really had.

If I would call a marina or airport looking for something, naturally the person you speak with is going to be skeptical. Everyone is to some extent. I quickly learned I couldn't walk up and say "I am a repo guy and I am here to take your customer's boat." I also had no desire or intention to be jumping fences, picking locks or doing anything else illegal. If I had taken the path of doing things illegally, I would have lost my license by now. I wasn't going to risk that. I had to be better than that.

Finding that 54-footer in Ft Lauderdale had gotten our foot in the door, but it was going to take a lot more than one successful case to establish our company. I decided to market to other lenders by asking for their toughest case. I felt good about getting this boat and wanted to prove to them, and myself, that this wasn't a fluke. A smaller bank in Tampa took me up on the offer.

I was excited to have the meeting with this executive from the bank. I had researched the bank and knew they had a decent sized portfolio of single and twin-engine airplanes on the books. I began my sales pitch and the banker was interested. Our location, our abilities, our track record. All in line with what the banker wanted from his vendors. I then told him I was willing to prove what I could do and asked for his toughest case. The banker laughed then yelled to his assistant to pull the file.

The banker handed me the file and told me they had been looking for a 1953 Tri-Pacer airplane for months. He said the plane had been near Orlando, which was my headquarters location. He told me a little bit about the debtor and wished me luck. This was a big chance with a new bank. I was ready.

This case took a lot of legwork. I found that the debtor had a home around Daytona, about 40 miles east of Orlando. I went there. This was a fly in community, so roads crossed with taxiways. When I approached a stop sign, I not only had to look for oncoming cars, but airplanes. It was a really cool place. In my research I found that his house was for sale. I called the realtor to get as much information as I could about the airplane, the debtor and anything else. The realtor let me know the owner was actually from Pennsylvania. She went on to mention the town and the debtor was one town over from me. I had some information to go on..

I called the debtor. I always like to have some tidbits of information I can use to either put the debtor at ease or have some leverage. In this case I decided to just ask where the plane was.

"I'm not telling you." He answered.

His flippant response got me angry. My initial reaction was to go after the debtor and press him hard. This is how I had been taught by my sponsor.

For some reason though, I knew this wouldn't work

with this older gentleman. I knew he was a veteran

and had been through a lot more than I could muster.

I decided to try and befriend him instead.

"I heard you are from Delaware County" I said.

"Yes I am. Lived there for 58 years before

moving here." He said, the tone of his voice already

softer.

"Do you know Chris Hassett**?" I asked.

(Chris was not actually the friends name. As you

might know from following the show, I have to change

names to protect people. Chris is actually a good

friend of mine whose name I always use on the show.

He knows and likes that I do that.)

"Yeah, I do. I did some work with Chris. How

do you know him?"

And just like that we were friends. We spent some time exchanging some names and stories. I asked him again where the plane was. He was still hesitant. He told me he was very sick and didn't have much time left. He didn't want this airplane loan causing a problem for his family when he was gone. My tone completely changed upon hearing this. I became empathetic and told him I would work with him to make sure he wasn't a burden.

"Listen. Let me help you get this thing off your hands. You aren't flying it. You can worry about the deficiency later." I explained.

He thought about it for a bit. Finally, he responded. "OK. I will tell you where it is, but you're not going to fly it."

I took that as a challenge, at first. I told him I would determine whether I would fly it or not, not him.

Then he told me where it was. Based on his instructions, I traveled to Ohio. Sure enough, hanging from the rafters of a popular steak house, was my airplane. The engine was removed, but the tail number was still visible. I had successfully located the airplane. The bank laughed it off and was very impressed that we found it. 11 years and about 40 repos later we still do some work for them.

I also found out pretty quickly that I needed to know my partners' trigger points. Different guys get upset by different things. You have all seen the great Danny Thompson at work. Danny is very calm…until he cannot be any more. His trigger point really, is someone threatening us or our job. I also learned that once he is angry, there is no point in me trying to calm things down. Danny will handle things his way. It will be intellectual and powerful. I say intellectual, because Danny always knows what he is doing and why he is doing it when he feels threatened. He doesn't waste energy, words or time. So when Danny gets mad, I merely point at the offender and say "He is all yours now. You are going to get what you have coming to you."

I always laugh about the pilot who has done the most repos with me. Trever Otto has been with me since 2006 and he is as cool and relaxed as can be. He was about 22 when he started working with me, so naturally people questioned his experience. That drove Trever nuts. He had thousands of hours in the air by the time he was 20 years old. He would never brag, but if someone did not give him the respect he deserved, he had a line he became famous for.

The first few times Trever gave his line, I honestly didn't notice. Then we went to a smaller airport in Michigan for a Mooney M20 Bravo. The

Bravo has a longer body, so handling is a little different. More importantly, the landing can be very difficult for less experienced pilots. Trever and I had no issue repossessing the airplane. We then took it to the FBO to get fuel and the manager there started asking why we had the airplane. I cleared everything up with him and then he asked who was flying the plane. Trever calmly answered that he was. The manager looked him up and down and questioned Trever. This did not sit well. "I don't mean to be a d!@% but..." And the line was born. I harassed Trever the rest of the day about that and brought it up so many times since then.

You get to know how people react to stress in this job. I always felt I was the crew chief and I believed it was my responsibility to know how everyone would react to difficult circumstances. I also strongly believe it is my job to make light of any line, comment, quirk or reaction that may show up. Humor in tight situations can make all of the difference. I use it when I can.

So what makes me panic? I will tell you. I went on a double airplane repo in Michigan. I wanted to repo both airplanes and fly commercially, so brought two pilots out. Tom Huntington has done hundreds of repos with me, so I asked him. I told him to get a pilot friend for the other one. He brought a tremendous Swiss pilot friend with him. His name was Andrea, pronounced An-DRE-uh. Not like the more common woman's name. We got into Detroit at about 10 am and were able to get the 2 repos done by 6 PM or so. The Pistons were playing the Orlando Magic in a playoff game in Detroit, so I called one of my best friends, Michael Forde who works for the Magic, where I should go. He pointed us to a great sports bar across the street from the stadium

When we arrived, the place was empty. I wasn't worried though. Tom and Andrea were about 23 years old, so they wanted something cold and frosty. We sat and enjoyed our meal and then the game ended. This bar began to fill up with happy Pistons fans, all in their young 20s. I mean happy. So the three of us stayed and laughed at some of the activity in the bar and left.

The next night I am home and go upstairs to watch a baseball game in my bedroom. My wife comes upstairs and sternly asks "Who is Andrea?" I panicked. My heart raced. I started sweating. I lost my breath. I had no idea what she was talking about. "I don't know. Why?" I muttered. "You got a text that says Thanks for the beer and good time from Andrea." And then it hit me. She had pronounced it as the female name. I went on a stream of information that lasted far longer than she wanted it to. She kept saying ok, but I kept going. She never looks at my phone, but this night she walked past and saw the name. She wanted to be sure it wasn't anything critical. It almost ended in a 911 call for me.

The lessons come in all ways, shapes and sizes. I have tried to learn as many as I could. I still have many, many more to learn but I am happy to admit I have learned many, many along the way.

CHAPTER 5: *Close Calls*

My friends always give me a hard time because so much of my work sends me to tropical locations.

"It must be tough" one of them will say, "having to go down to Jamaica for work."

Let me tell you. There is a big difference between going to Jamaica for vacation and going down to repossess a twin-engine airplane likely being used to transport drugs. I don't get to see the resorts, the beach or the bars. I don't get days off. I work from sun up until I am done. I don't think I have ever gone to a resort swimming pool. When I am there, no matter how cool the location, I am there to work.

On the rare occasions when I am at a resort location, I am not there long enough to enjoy any of the amenities. I go there, take the asset I need to take and get out of there as quickly and quietly as possible. I may have to pack suntan lotion for a lot of my business trips, but over the years I have seen my fair share of dicey situations.

Now please do not misunderstand me. I am not complaining. There are times when I have been face to face with an angry debtor or times I have had to deal with guys that will cussed and threatened me. There were even people who felt the need to lift their shirts to show me what they had tucked into their belts. The truth is, if someone wants to shoot me for taking their boat or airplane, I am going to walk away and come back another day to get it. No case is worth that. Walking away on one day doesn't mean I have walked away for good.

My wife always says I have a natural ability to calm people down. When it comes to confrontations, I can go into a near trance. I am not thinking about the dangers. I am just focused on calming this person in front of me and getting my repo done. Once the situation calms down, that is when I really feel the adrenaline surging. It gets so intense sometimes I can taste it. It can make my entire body shake. Literally get the shakes. It is that feeling that some people live for and others avoid.

I have seen a lot of close calls over the years. One of my favorite cases happened in New Jersey. Go figure, right? I was asked to repo three airplanes that turned out to be flight school planes. This meant that when we took the airplanes, we were basically shutting down the airport's flight school. I knew this could make the case that much more difficult. This is one of the reasons I didn't like taking flight school planes. The other reason is these planes are often beaten up pretty good and the managers of these planes are masters of keeping the planes in the air without overspending for maintenance.

On this particular case, I had two of my regular pilots with me. Trever and Duke Simily. These two were good friends and really good pilots. I had met Trever when he was a student at Embry Riddle and he had worked a case with me that went pretty crazy. While he didn't handle himself as well on that case as I would have hoped, more on this later, I could tell he was an excellent pilot. As things got busier for IRG, Trever brought in Duke and a couple others from ERU. Duke was a Staten Island guy, so knew he could handle anything that might come up in Jersey. I always appreciated Duke's confidence and humor. We had similar attitudes, which made it fun for me.

We made it a point to get to the airport early. This was shortly after being on the _Wall Street Journal_ and that meant I had a news crew in tow. This was just another wrinkle I liked to throw into my repos. As soon as we got there, we were able see two of our airplanes were grounded. We immediately changed the plan. We would just fly the remaining one out and come back to tow the other two. I was keeping an eye out for any problems while the pilots took their time inspecting the airplane. In between, the news people were asking questions, so I was busy. As soon as the inspection was complete, Trever and Duke said we were ready to go. The news crew would not be flying, so I told them where to go to get some footage of the takeoff.

As Trever and Duke were running up the plane and taxiing us to the runway, I noticed an old man type pull up to the flight school office in his white Cadillac. He gave a quick nod to us and went inside. This didn't feel right. I told the guys to pick it up so we didn't run into problems. They told me they would take the airplane to the side of the threshold where we would be out of sight and do the rest of the checks there.

They finished the run up and the logbook checks and told me they were ready. I gave them the thumbs up and they began to turn onto the runway. Just then, I noticed the white Caddy pulling out of the parking lot in a hurry. I told the guys they were onto us and they had to get moving. They began moving down the runway and we could see the Caddy on the taxiway coming hot for us. "This could be it." I thought. The gap was closing and I knew the car could make a right at any time to cut us off. I believed he was crazy enough to try to cut us off.

"What is he doing?" Duke yelled

"No idea." I shouted back. "Guess he is trying to stop us. Get this thing off the ground!"

Trever, just as cool as could be, lifted the

airplane off the ground as the Caddy did turn into the

runway about 100 feet in front of us. We cleared the

car by what felt like inches. Trever never broke a

sweat or showed any signs of stress at all. Duke and

I bantered back and forth about how close that was

and how crazy that FBO manager was. I called the

news crew when we landed. They said they caught it

all, but wouldn't show more than they needed to.

Then there was the repo of a newer Robinson

R22 helicopter I did at Compton airport outside of Los

Angeles. I was already hesitant and cautious just

because of where it was. I had heard so much on the

news over the years, I just didn't know what to expect.

As is my nature on these repos, I was expecting the

worst.

I went to the airport and was amazed. The

airport was beautiful and they had many artifacts and

decorations celebrating the Tuskegee Airmen and other great accomplishments in aviation by African American aviators. I also saw they were holding a class for about 8 kids. They were pre-teens and young teens and they were learning about aviation. It was one of the coolest things I have seen offered at an airport

While there was a great deal of activity in the airport, there was none outside when we walked onto the field. I walked around for a few seconds and was feeling a whole lot better about my surroundings. The helicopter was white, so I was able to spot it pretty quickly. It was only a couple of years old, but it looked nearly new when we pulled up on it. This was great news.

The pilot immediately began doing the pre-flight check and it went quickly. He was preparing for the flight to a small airport near San Diego, where we would sell the airplane.   The helicopter had flown in the last day or two and it was a newer unit, which made us both feel better. We had planned to drop me off at a municipal airport a few miles away and then the pilot would continue.

I joked with the pilot about this repo being the last of the day and me getting a nice dinner and some sleep before heading home to Philadelphia. I was looking to see if anyone noticed us and I saw no activity at all. We were ready, so we jumped in the airplane. The pilot put the key in and it cranked right up. He gave me the thumbs up and said it felt great. I was excited about what I had seen in the airport and to be getting a normal night in LA. Just as we started lifting off I heard an odd sound. POP! I asked the pilot what it was, thinking it was the engine.

"It's not the helicopter" he said.

Just then I realized my worst nightmare.

Someone was shooting at us from the ground. I

couldn't see anyone, but there was no doubt

someone was not happy to see us in this helicopter

now.

"We are getting shot at!!" I yelled to the pilot.

"HOLD ON!" he exclaimed and he began

maneuvers with this helicopter that I wasn't prepared

for. A couple of zigs and zags and everything calmed

down. We got out safely, but the ride was really

scary.

I wrote about exotic locations before and I have

been to several. My first time in the US Virgin

Islands, was to do a repo in St Croix. I was working

for a really small bank in New England. I knew they

had very little to secure, but they were paying me to

go to St. Croix, so I was going. I was trying to take

back an old Cessna Cardinal that was there. It turned out that the owner was a guy from Connecticut and he had taken the plane there. I came to find out the debtor was illegally using the airplane for site seeing tours. The maintenance on this airplane was poor at best.

I went to the airport early in the morning with my pilot. We were able to get onto the field and found our airplane sitting at the front corner of airport. It was obvious at first inspection that this airplane wouldn't be flying to Florida today. I had to come up with another plan. I went down to Bohlke Air on the field and asked them about providing the maintenance. They agreed.

Bohlke Air has become a friend of IRG over the years, as has the Bohlke family. This was my 1st experience with Mr. Bohlke and he exuded class and respectability. When I told him which airplane I was getting, he said they could do the work and advised me to call the local police. I heeded his advice and shortly after, met the officer inside of the Bolhlke offices. I explained what I was doing to the officer. He offered to drive me up to the airplane to inform the debtor, who we were told had shown up. This was a lot easier than it would have been in the States.

As the officer drove us out, we were in casual conversation. This changed quickly though, when we saw the Cardinal running up its engines on the threshold of the runway. The debtor was trying to steal the airplane back and take it off of the island. The police officer didn't like this move at all, so he went speeding down the runway after the plane. The officer was fired up. Unfortunately, the officer's ingenious plan had him turning the car to block the airplane with me nearest to the propeller. If that debtor decided to take off, I was in deep trouble. Fortunately, that didn't happen.

Angry debtors aren't the only thing I have to deal with. The bankers understand that the longer their assets are with the debtors, the more the value potentially decreases. So, they often put aggressive timelines on us. These deadlines can require more aggressive responses to problems. Once, this led to us repossessing a Citation jet and attempting to deliver the airplane to the banker at a regional airport. When we were trying to contact the tower for permission to land, the pilots noticed the radios weren't working.

The pilot in charge gave me a couple of choices. We can try to land without contact, which could lead to a head on collision and would cause a lot of trouble for us if we landed. Or, we can turn back, leaving the banker standing on the tarmac without his airplane.

For a few tense moments, we were faced with a choice of giving up our commission or trying to land this jet with no ground contact. We looked frantically for some way to resolve the problem. Luckily, we were able to find a back-up radio unit stashed underneath the seat just in time, narrowly avoiding the risk of a collision.

Sometimes, the close calls have little to do with the repo. One such incident happened near Lake Okeechobee in Florida. Danny and I were there filming the Cessna 310 repossession for season 1 of the show. This is the episode where the debtor came after us with the shovel. Not surprisingly, the debtor lived in a shady looking neighborhood. We weren't having any luck, so finding the airplane, so we had to go to the house. We ended up finding restaurant receipts for an airport about 35 miles from the house, which led to the repo.

What you didn't see was the neighbor's house. We were scouting the neighborhood and wanted to talk to neighbors to see if they knew anything. We went onto the porch, with a camera guy, to knock. Danny took a step on the porch and yelled "HALT! Do NOT move." I had no idea what was going on, but stopped immediately. Danny then told us to slowly walk away from the porch and go to the car. I still didn't know what was going on, but Danny was very clear, so I walked to the car with the camera guy. Danny looked in the front window, then came to the car.

"What was that Danny?" I asked

"Crack house" Danny answered.

Turned out, Danny felt a loose floor board when he stepped up. Not just a loose board though, one that was removed and replaced as is often seen in these situations. It was a great way to hide drugs. When Danny looked in the window, he saw squatters in there. If we had knocked on the door, anything could have happened. The residents likely wouldn't have offered us coffee though. Talk about a close call. This could have been one of the closest and it didn't even involve a debtor or an asset.

There have been many close calls over the years. When you handle over 2,000 cases in 11 years, that will happen. I like to think some good planning, along with some luck, has helped keep me and my team safe over the years.

CHAPTER 6: *A Citation, A Challenger and One Furious Pro Football Player*

When it comes to high-intensity situations, there is one job that beats them all. It may be my favorite case of all. It had great investigative work, an awesome confrontation, lots of money on the line and the pressure of a new client. It is the story that seems to be the one people like the most at parties as well. It is the story that had it all.

I had been talking to a bank in Georgia for a month or two about doing work for them in 2008. There is always an excitement and pressure that comes with a new client. Finally, they told me they had two jets they thought they wanted picked up and asked if they thought I could get them. They told me the last known location was Orlando International Airport, which was right down the road from me. I told the banker I was sure I could get them, so we got the orders. She asked me to report to them regularly as everyone at the bank was new to repossessing airplanes.

The total value of the two airplanes, a Citation and a Challenger, was about $7,000,000, so this was a really big case for us. The bank indicated they had a decent sized portfolio of similar airplanes and may need us again if this one went well. Adding this client and these cases was a big boost for IRG.

I immediately called one of my favorite pilots, David Larson, for this case. I figured he would be perfect. Dave is a very smart and extremely capable pilot who was incredibly calm under pressure. Not only could he fly one of the airplanes, but he knew everyone in aviation in Orlando. He was bound to know some people who could help us get the airplane.

I began with the investigation and found some things out of the gate that were concerning. The debtor said he was involved in some very high-end, high-profile businesses. He owned an exotic rental car company in Central Florida, for example. As we dug deeper, we were able to determine that he had some other projects he was working on off the record. These projects were in Venezuela, Nicaragua and Mexico to name a few.

We also were able to determine that he used these airplanes to make regular trips overseas. We didn't learn of any business connections there, so we feared the worst. Why would someone need a Challenger to go from South Florida to South America to Europe? And why would they need to go each month? To be safe, we tracked the movements of the airplanes for two weeks or so to see if there were any patterns. There were. The Citation was parked and the Challenger was due back in Orlando, with another flight out 36 hours after it landed. The window to repossess both together was small.

With that in mind, we decided to make our move late one Wednesday night in January. We figured the airplanes would be in a hangar and would be locked so we planned accordingly. Dave was not available this night as he was flying for someone else, so I went to the airport that night with one of Trever's young pilot friends, Tom Huntington. Tom was a great resource for us because, not only could he fly any number of different airplanes, but he was also a mechanic. Tom went on a lot of cases with me for this reason and I definitely wanted him around when we got the airplanes to do a quick look at the Citation.

When we got the airport, we noticed that it was very slow in there. This was a good thing for us. I did a quick survey inside and outside the fixed based operation (FBO) and saw that it was a good time to go. I approached the woman at the counter, a young woman who looked to be a bit less experienced, and told her what I was there for. I was prepared for all of the follow up questions, but did not get any. She led us directly to the airplane in the hangar. This was surprisingly easy.

When we got to the airplane, I saw it was locked with an "unpickable" lock. I had worked on legally picking locks for some time and actually got pretty good at it, but my sidekick at the time fancied himself as a first-rate lock picker, so he went at it. All the while, Tom the pilot was harassing him.

"You'll never get it. It's unpickable. You are wasting your time." He kept saying.

I leaned in and asked below all of the noise. "What do you think? Can you get it?"

He quietly answered "I already know which way the tumblers go." At that, I was confident he would get it. I went to another part of the hangar and called the repo into the police and then the bank. As I was leaving a message for the bank, my sidekick completed the pick and started screaming and dancing towards the pilot. I completed my call, while laughing at the theatrics and proceeded to the now open airplane. It was in great shape. We were halfway done.

We went back at 6:30 the next morning with Dave. He had coordinated this part of the repo, having pilots in place to move the airplanes once we secured the 2nd one. We pulled into the airport parking lot and started surveying the area. At that, my phone rings and it is the bank. I answered quickly and heard Amy from the bank on the other end.

"Ken, are y'all ok?" She asked in a panicked southern drawl. "Did you get shot? What's going on?"

"Amy, we are fine. Everything went smoothly on the Citation and we are moving in on the Challenger." I answered her.

"Well y'all had me going crazy here. I heard all the noise in your message and thought y'all were getting shot at." She said in a relieved and slightly annoyed tone. I apologized for scaring her and told her I would call when the job was completed.

I asked the new person at the counter about the Challenger. She asked who I was and I told her my name and let her know I was the one who had the Citation and I needed that one too. She said the plane was in the hangar on the south end of the field. She said it was being prepared for a flight later in the day. We had to move fast if we were going to move the planes before anyone showed up.

We raced over to the Challenger and spoke to someone at the hangar who let us onto the field. We moved straight to the Challenger and saw some line people tending to the airplane. I told them I needed to airplane towed to the FBO and the lineman agreed. While I waited, I noticed a small, balding guy peeking out from the hangar. He was as shifty as could be and made me very uncomfortable. When he saw me looking his way, he ducked back inside the hangar. Just then, the tug arrived and began working on hooking up the Challenger. Dave, my sidekick and I jumped in the car and went back to the FBO.

I went in and asked the girl at the counter to pull the Citation out and prepare it for a flight to my airport. She agreed and we went outside to prepare for a quick exit. Dave called his pilots and they began moving towards us from a location very near us. It was on and we had to get out before anyone came to interfere with this great plan.

The planes were both staged within a couple of minutes of each other and we had both Citation pilots ready. I told them to begin doing the inspections of the airplane to prepare for the 4-minute flight. I instructed the person at the counter to send out the other two pilots when they arrived. My sidekick and I would stand guard and keep an eye out while this was going on.

A few minutes later, I noticed the shifty guy from the hangar walking around outside the FBO smoking a cigarette. He was pacing furiously. I yelled to the pilots

"How are you guys doing? Are we ready? We may have company soon!"

And just as the words left my mouth, my sidekick and I noticed a yellow sports car racing across the field from the hangar where we found the Challenger. He was coming right over to us. We both knew what this meant.

"Get in the plane and lock yourselves in!" I yelled to the pilots.

They misunderstood though. They thought I had said strap yourselves in. They took that to mean take a look at the systems. The first pilot got in the left seat, but Dave hung outside with us until the PIC (pilot in charge) was ready.

The yellow car pulled up and out from the car stepped this hulking man who came barreling towards us. He was big and strong. He looked to be in phenomenal shape. We later found out this person was a former NFL player and he looked it.

This intimidating figure loudly informed us that he was a pilot for these airplanes, so his job was on the line. He then told us he was boarding the Citation.

I stood my ground.

"This is my plane." I said. "It's been repo'd."

The pilot insisted I let him board the airplane. For reasons known only to him, he really wanted to retrieve his headset valued at about $125. He stormed at me, spewing profanities the entire time. I was risking the repo legally at this point so, when he approached the steps, I boarded the airplane first and warned the pilot.

He grabbed his headset and a couple of meaningless books that were his. He cursed and threatened both of us. Something wasn't right about this guy, so we gave him space and didn't engage him. This was just getting started though.

As he deplaned, he saw Dave standing on the ground, his back to the airplane. The former NFL player lunged at him from the 2nd step and gave him a vicious two-hand shiver from behind, sending Dave flying. Dave caught this shot without any advance notice from this huge guy and it sent him about 15 feet. We had to do something quickly to restore order and get these airplanes.

This guy was losing his mind. He had veins bulging from his arms, which was not unusual. He also had them bulging from his forehead, which stunned me briefly. I also noticed his eyes were glazing and he was sweating profusely. Far more than he should be on a beautiful winter morning in Florida, where temperatures were in the low to mid 60's. It was then I realized he on something bad.

This would just make the task that much more difficult.

My experience as an emergency responder kicked in. I calmed myself quickly and began barking orders to make sure jobs were done properly and get the momentum back on our side. I saw a line person standing outside, watching the events.

"Call 911" I yelled to them. They responded quickly to go inside.

"Get him away from here." I yelled to my sidekick, who was standing pretty close to the crazed pilot. The sidekick heard and began challenging him. "You want a piece of me, come over here." I heard him say. Not exactly the route I wanted, but it was effective.

I ran over to check up on Dave. Dave is aneasy-going guy, but there is another side to him that surprised me the first time I saw it. He has a real toughness about him. His toughness was incredibly evident at this time. He was pretty angry about the cheap shot and wanted to get back at the guy. But Dave was smarter than that. He wouldn't get him back physically. He would get him back in a much more profound way.

"You ok Dave?" I asked him.

"Yeah. I'm fine. Guy gave me a good shot though." He said with a smirk.

"Are you hurt anywhere?" I asked, wanting to be sure I wasn't getting a husband and dad hurt.

"Ken, I'm fine. But we have him now." He said confidently.

"What the hell are you talking about Dave?"

"Once the police get here, I will use this against him to get the logbooks." Dave responded.

Well look at that. Dave took a pretty vicious blow from a massive and strong individual and he is thinking about getting the logbooks. As you may recall from the television show, the logbooks can be worth anywhere from 20% to 50% of the airplanes value in a resale. Dave knew this and he was willing to use his leverage to get us the books. It wasn't something he had to do, and it certainly wasn't something he needed to be thinking about at that time. But he was and I really appreciated it.

The police showed up and seemed less than interested. A repossession is a civil matter, meaning the police are not supposed to assist or support us in any way, and they were making sure they were not assisting us. As the officer began talking to me, I noticed the pilot sneaking quietly into the FBO lounge. I stressed to the officer that the issue wasn't a contested repo. It was the assault by the pilot. The officer agreed to talk to the pilot.

When we went in, we saw something so strange it still sticks with me. He was in this weird, almost meditative state. Still sweating profusely and his eyes looked to be rolling in the back of his head. The officer weakly attempted to speak with the pilot, but he wasn't responding. After a minute or so, the officer motioned for us to go outside with him.

He told us he would work with us, but made it pretty clear he didn't want to arrest this guy at this point. Dave spoke up and told him he wouldn't press charges if the guy gave us the logbooks for both airplanes. The officer understood the deal and said, once the pilot came to, he would present the offer.

About two hours passed. At this point, I was there with my sidekick, Dave and the 3 other pilots, who just wanted to fly. I also called Glenda down with a truck because the logbooks would probably need some room to transport. The officer gave us a call and in we went to talk to the pilot.

I can only assume that the pilot was off of his crazy high, because now he was the nicest, most social guy in the room. The officer explained our offer to the pilot. He immediately accepted. The officer went with us to his office to collect the logbooks. Luckily, we had Glenda's truck because there were more than 30 plastic tubs filled with paperwork. I carried them out to the vehicles for transport and gave the thumbs up to send Glenda and the pilots home.

The now sober pilot then showed us pictures of the people he had flown for, including one President. He showed us pictures of him in his NFL uniform and told stories. We hung around for another 20-30 minutes listening. At that, we left and celebrated a great day and a better story. After a day like that I was happy to have repo'd both planes I was hired to find. More importantly I was thankful that everyone was going to be going home to their families safe and sound.

About three weeks later, I was approached at another central Florida airport and a pilot friend asked if we had repo'd the two jets. I told him we did. He asked if I had heard about the pilot, which I had not. He told me he heard he was locked up on drug charges. I never checked to see if it was true, but after that day I didn't feel I needed to.

CHAPTER 7: *Repo Dad*

This job can be difficult in many ways. One of the most difficult things is trying to balance my family life with the business. There have been many, many times when I have missed important events or milestones.

I put together parties when each season premiered as a way of recognizing and thanking all of the people who had helped me in some way get to that point. For the first season, I invited a friend who coached basketball with me. We were coaching a team of 3rd grade boys we named the Tar Heels (always my team's name as a die-hard North Carolina fan) when I was filming the first season, so I wanted him there.

In the premiere episode of *Airplane Repo*, I was shown tracking down a $180,000 Beech Baron

58. The episode tracked me and my new partner, Danny Thompson chasing and tracking this plane for weeks going from Phoenix to New Mexico to Canada and all places in between. In the end, after playing cat and mouse across several airports, Danny and I finally caught up with the debtor while he was fueling his airplane. He was trying to make another get-away. Danny shut down the gas line while he was pumping. This allowed us to keep the guy grounded and we were able to recover the airplane. It was a fun repo and I think a solid opening episode of the show.

After the episode aired, I yelled over to to my friend.

"Hey. You remember that one time I red-eyed in for that game?"

"Yeah. I do." he said.

"Well, that's where I was coming from. That job right there." I said.

He couldn't believe it. Showing people exactly where I was and what I was doing gives them a much better idea of what my days and weekends are actually like. Everybody thinks I am nuts for doing what I do. Not just the repos, but the running around like crazy to make events. But, as I reminded my friend, my 9-year-old son had 24 points and 12 steals in that game. It is a great memory that I will have forever. Hopefully my son will too. If I had missed that, I never would have forgiven myself.

There was another time I was filming for season 3 and I was in California. Jimmy was now 11 and I was coaching his baseball team, but would be missing this one on a job. My wife sends me an excited text with a video. My first thought is always panic, but this time it was to tell me that Jimmy had hit his first ever homerun over the fence. I was crushed.

Crushed. I literally told the crew I needed to grab a

coffee before I could get back to filming.

His next game came on the following Saturday

and I was at home. I joked with him before the game

that it was ok to hit one with me there. He said "OK

Dad. 2nd at bat." I laughed. He came up for his

second at bat and I was coaching 3rd base, as I

always did. On the second pitch he swings and

launches a rocket, over the fence and into a

neighbor's yard. As he rounds first base, he looks at

me on third base and puts up two fingers and mouths

"Second at bat." It still gives me a good laugh. It is

for moments like that. That is why I work so hard to

see every game.

Lots of people where I live only know me from

coaching their kids' team or maybe from seeing me at

some school event. This was especially true before

the show aired. Before that, they might have had an idea of what I was doing for a living and may have thought it was kind of cool. I think the TV show changed their impression of me and my job a little bit. After they see the show, some will come up to me and say "Wow. I didn't know you did that!" Yes, that's what I have been trying to tell you!

My kids don't really understand the full extent of my job, which is the way I prefer it. Besides, I am just Dad to them anyway. They never let on that they are the least bit impressed or affected that I am even on TV. Unless I am on the field with them coaching one of their games, at this point they are pretty much bored with me. Even then, I am still pretty boring to them now.

It has been funny to see and hear their friends' reactions though. My older son, David, was going to his 8th grade dance and my wife and I went to his friend's house to get pictures. There were probably 30 kids there, all dressed in suits and dresses. All looking very grown up. A couple of them come over to me and started talking. One, who I have known since he was about 8, says "I google you in class. You are worth more than Lil Wayne is!" David is there and he has a smirk on while shaking his head. "He looks you up all the time Dad." I just laughed.

Recently I had a discussion with a 15-year-old on David's baseball team about what I do…during a game. Every answer I gave he laughed and told me how awesome he thought it was. I had to stop his questioning to get him to go pitch. I thought that would end it, but as soon as he came in, he picked it up where he left off.

I wonder still how this affects my kids. My girls are older, so they just enjoy it. My older daughter even had me speak at her college and she sat in for it. The boys seem to like it, but don't want to act like they do. The kind of just go with it.

Being involved with my kids' activities is by far the most important thing to me. As a teenager, after I got sick, I started coaching youth sports alongside my Dad and after that I never stopped. I have rescheduled jobs in order to make my kids' games or other important activities. I want to be there for them and for all the other kids too.

I coached all of my daughters' teams when they were growing up and now I am able to coach my sons as well. This wasn't always the case though. For the first 6 years or so that I owned IRG, I didn't coach my kids. I had to miss practices, games, fun time in the yard or street. Most of it. That used to make me crazy, so I committed to doing everything I could, as long as I could.

One time, I was in Van Nuys, California working on a case. We were with producers who were trying to film a sizzle reel for us. The plane I was after was worth about $275,000. I was not yet used to having a camera crew with me and they made it a bit more difficult. The cameras brought a lot more attention, especially in LA, but I was able to repo the plane and get the pilot to begin taking it back to Orlando. The cross-country trip would take about 3 days in this airplane. While I was there, I scheduled a meeting with a bank I wanted to work with.

"So you want the big stuff?" the department head asked me. I answered affirmatively. He said he was willing to give me a shot and he decided to give us a $5.3 million Citation that was in Orlando. Before I could even celebrate on the inside, he hit me with a catch. They wanted it secured by the end of the week and it was already Tuesday. I had to fly back east, which would take one day, so in reality we were already halfway through the week.

This was a big deal. First, this was a big case worth a lot of money. Also, as you can tell, new clients are a huge deal for us. There is a limited number of potential clients, so getting one and keeping them are critical. So, if we performed on this one, we could expect more cases to come behind it. These pressures were ones I had dealt with before.

The only problem was, my older son David, had his first ever playoff baseball game. So now, instead of flying home for it, as had been planned, I was diverting for the repossession. I was dealing with a lot of guilt, while trying to focus on a big job. I had promised to be Dad first and now I was not living up to that promise. I tried to justify flying home to see his game and going on Thursday for the jet, but I knew that was not a possibility. I had to get the plane first.

We landed with a plan to do to the airplane after the company that owned the airplane closed at 6 pm. We landed just after 4, so we had some time before we had to move. We got our things and grabbed a quick dinner before we headed over. When dinner was done, we got in the car and I saw someone walking into the restaurant. I couldn't believe my eyes. It was the shifty guy from the Citation, Challenger repo. "That's not a good sign." I said. It shouldn't have surprised us since he did work at the airport, but it did. We stayed low in case he was involved in the airplane we were going for that night.

We had an address of where the airplane would be, so we began driving towards it. Dave Larson was with us. As I mentioned before, Dave knows everyone in the aviation community in this area. He had spoken to a pilot friend about where the airplane was located and the possibility of entering the hangar. He told us there was a door on the side and we should enter there. If we needed a code, we were to call him and he would provide it. He had an office in the hangar, so it would all be legit. We were set.

This was going to happen at Orlando International Airport. This meant we needed to be prepared for the highest security level possible. When we got to the address, we saw the hangar was old and beat up. I remembered being here for the Challenger from last chapter. That was in the hangar next door. This was not starting off too well. We parked and walked to the door and, to our surprise, the door was propped open. How great was this? Maybe I was wrong about the bad vibe I felt at the restaurant.

We again had a camera crew that was filming our every move. We all walked in the hangar, down a long hallway to where the planes were stored. Along the way, we saw a guy in a small office with a weather hat on. "That must be who propped the door open." I told the camera. On we went. We were not seeing any resistance at all.

When we ended the hallway, we saw about 8 airplanes stacked in the hangar. There were planes of various shapes, sizes and types. I knew what I was looking for, so quickly perused the area looking for my Citation. After looking around for a few seconds, I found it. Yachtsee baby! There was my big payday.

I was so focused on looking for the airplane that I didn't notice the two guys in the hangar. They were airport employees who were preparing planes to be moved from the hangar. My airplane was blocked in and I needed help to get mine out anyway, so I was going to try to talk them into clearing my plane for transport. I walked out confidently and asked

"Hey guys. Are you here to get my plane out for me?"

"Which one is yours?" the manager asked.

"That one. I need to take it out tonight." I said as I pointed to the Citation.

"Nobody told us about it. Did you call it in?" he asked.

"I called Tony." I said, remembering the manager's name from the last time we were here to repo the Citation and Challenger.

"Do you have any paperwork?" he asked.

I remember seeing this line guy from the last repo and remembered he was very helpful. I thought

I would go for it right here. I then flashed my repo letter to him. His eyes lit up when he realized what it was.

"I remember you!" He said.

He said it in a friendly tone, so felt we might be in good hands. He asked his partner to stay with us and then went to go call Tony. We all agreed that Tony would have to give the authorization to release the airplane and figured I would be talking to him soon. We received permission from the airport employee who was with us to enter the Citation. He approved so we all began looking at the airplane and taking pictures in preparation for finalizing the repossession.

By this time, my son's playoff game had begun. My wife hates when I do this, but I started texting her for updates. I wanted scores, inning and how my son was doing. While waiting for her responses, I called the repossession into the police. I got my report number and was well on my way. Dave was doing the physical inspection, reviewing the POH (Pilot's Operating Handbook) and was ready to do the run-ups. We were moving along quickly.

I then noticed the line guy coming back to us, but he had a far different demeanor than I expected. He told us he called Tony and left a message. He then told us he called airport security and they were heading over to talk about it. I asked why he went behind us like that and he said because he couldn't get through to Tony and we didn't belong there. And so it began.

"Dodgers winning 5-2 after 2 innings. David has a double and 2 RBI. He is hitting again next inning." Was the text I received from my wife. The

Dodgers were David's team, so they were up. A quick fist pump and then back to the new nightmare.

The next thing I know, here comes the head of TSA for the airport along with 4 agents. Then 4 police cars pulled up to the hangar. The TSA wanted to lock us up in the worst way. The hangar door was open when we entered, which meant we had access to the tarmac. For that reason, we needed to be escorted by a badged employee throughout. He was on us and wouldn't let go. We were being detained by TSA.

"David got another double and knocked in a run. We are up 9-2. David up again soon." Another text to break up the chaos. This really helped to keep me calm during what should have been a stressful time.

One of the officers walked up to me and asked for my paperwork, which I provided. She kept telling me the TSA couldn't do anything to us, but wanted to detain us. My paperwork checked out and my call-in was verified, so legally I was fine. I just couldn't leave yet.

"Why are you holding us here?" I asked.

"Because you have to have a badged employee with you at all times and you didn't." he yelled back.

"Isnt that guy badged?" I asked as I pointed to a line guy who hadn't left our side.

"Yes. But we need to check all of you out and I am especially concerned about HIM!" he yelled as he pointed at Dave.

"David got a single and knocked in 2. We are blowing them out now. He is up again in a second." My wife texted, not knowing how tense things were with me.

I now knew they had no reason to hold us, so we decided to push this along. This is a strategy that can work and can blow up for us too. It was time though.

"Dave, call our attorney. Right now. He admitted he has no reason to hold us. The police verified the paperwork. I want him out here now." I said.

I then went to the police who were on our side and asked them to push things along. They knew we had a badged employee and this was now just an embarrassed guy trying to throw his perceived power around. I wasn't having it.

"David with another double and RBI. OMG Ken, I wish you were here to see this."

My son was 4-4 with 6 RBIs in his first playoff game and I was being detained by some guy trying to save face. I was so proud of my son, so filled with guilt for missing it and I was hot, tired and annoyed. I was through.

"Listen dude, you got nothing on us. We had a badged employee, this is a legal repo and we are moving." I said. The police officers gave me a relieved look, so I knew I was ok. Just then Tony, the airport manager showed up.

"What's going on here Tony? This guy is getting ready to get sued for holding us and you know we are legit!" I said.

Tony pulled me aside and said he was furious with his line guy for calling in TSA. He told me he had to ask for some paperwork in front of everyone to help save face. I agreed and then presented the documents that he requested. I never have a problem providing any paperwork an airport needs.

The TSA Supervisor, in one last stand to try show their authority told us we had 30 minutes to get wheels up, or they wouldn't allow us to leave.

"Game over. We won 21-6. David ended up with 5 hits." Now, I could relax because I knew all was good at home. We had already begun the inspections and checks, so had the airplane pulled out.

15 minutes later, we were in the air for our 7-minute flight. As soon as the door closed, I called my son to congratulate him on an epic game. I then filmed some things for the crew quickly and landed. This day that started with a cross country flight was done. 18 hours later.

It was a great story and a great win. To be able to overcome all we were able to, was no small feat. The one thing that helped us emerge victorious is knowing the rules and following them. There were many things we could take pride in that night. At that moment though, I wasn't really concerned about that. My mind was a thousand miles away the whole time. Missing his game was a big deal. Maybe not to him, but to me. It wasn't what I really wanted to do that night. But this was my life as a "Repo Dad".

CHAPTER 8: *Working in Paradise*

One of the things I like the most about this job is the investigations. It is probably my favorite thing to do. The cases that require a lot of work to find are the ones I like the best. Another thing I love, is traveling to some incredible places. When I get both in one case, I am excited.

I got a call one October day from a very small bank in central Florida. They had a problem with a debtor who they were deeply invested in. I began working on the case and it led me to the Bahamas. It was a 120' yacht worth over $8 million. I did some work in the office, as always, and confirmed that the boat had recently been in the Bahamas. I found out the debtor's son was a criminal and had been arrested many times for drugs, assault, weapons and more. When I see this, I know I need to take another person with me.

I decided to take a friend from home with me. Grady's wife and my wife are best of friends and all of our kids are close. We see each other at baseball fields, birthday parties and the beach. He mentioned he would like to go on a case and I thought this was a good one for him. I told him I needed someone that was "quiet crazy." He knew exactly what I meant and said "Sounds like you found your guy." So I began filling him in on the case.

I had tracked the boat to a small inlet surrounded by concrete and condos. Grady and I flew into the Bahamas and took a cab to a hotel on the other side of the bay from where I knew the boat to be. I softened Grady up with a nice lunch and a beer, then went to check on my captain, Alex Sorice. He expected to arrive around 6 PM he said, so Grady and I hopped on a water taxi to go see if the boat was where I thought.

It was a spectacular day in the Bahamas. It was especially nice for two guys from Philly for the Monday after Thanksgiving. We both appreciated taking the water taxi for the 20-minute jaunt to the location, although I had some concern that the mega-yacht would be in place when we pulled around the bend. I was relieved and excited when I saw the huge vessel glistening in the sunlight. It was spectacular.

I asked the Bahamian driving the boat to pull up closer so I could see how it was sitting. It was docked in a way to make it extremely difficult to take it quickly. The nose and starboard side were against concrete walkway. The lines were tied properly and they were using bumpers along the sidewalks. These were good signs as it looked to be well cared for. I told the driver we were ok and asked him to return us to the restaurant, where we would wait for Alex.

Six o'clock came and went with no sign of Alex. I grew impatient and started blowing up his phone. Texts, calls, voicemails, all of it and no response. I was equal parts concerned and furious. This was an $8 million megayacht that was just sitting there and I couldn't get it. Finally, at about 7:30, Alex calls to tell me he just landed and is headed to me. He got out of the cab and it was plain to see that he wasn't moving any boat tonight.

"Ken, I ain't moving any boat tonight. Too dark and I need light to get out from where it is. I am going to the casino." He told me. As much as I hated to admit it, it was the right move. We talked it over for a few minutes more and decided to grab something to eat. We agreed to meet in the hotel lobby at 7 am sharp the next morning.

Grady and I are up and ready in plenty of time. We headed to the lobby at about 6:40 and I grabbed a coffee. It was a spectacular morning. It was sunny and warm with a comfortable breeze going. This truly was paradise. As you might imagine, Alex was late. He was always a shade late. He took the "island time" thing to heart. I sat outside and enjoyed the weather and my coffee for a few minutes. I looked at the boats moving effortlessly on the calm water. It was a great day to steal a boat and take it to the US.

At about 7:20, I noticed the sun getting blocked by something to my left. I turned to look and saw this massive yacht heading out of the inlet to the ocean. My heart sank and I lost my breath for a second. The sun glare made it impossible for me to make out the name on the boat, but I knew it was mine. I ran inside to tell Grady and we went together to get Alex.

I banged on his door ferociously and he finally answered in a stupor. His hair stood up like a troll doll. I was stunned for a second, then blurted out "Our yacht is on the run."

Alex immediately came to and was as alert and fresh as could be.

"What do you mean?" he asked.

"I just watched it head out the inlet and it is moving to open waters." I explained.

"I will meet you downstairs in 5 minutes" he promised.

This time Alex and his mechanic were on time. We all watched the boat for about 15 to 20 minutes. We determined the boat was either heading to the west end of the island, or Fort Lauderdale. The course didn't change, so we decided to track the boat and grab a really fast breakfast. At about 9 am, the boat broke off its course and started on a 278-degree heading. I will always remember that heading. This was what we were waiting for. The confirmation of where the boat was headed. It was going to Fort Lauderdale, FL.

We all grabbed our bags and I booked 4 tickets on a 16-seat airplane at 10:20 am. We jumped in a too small cab and went off on a bumpy jaunt to the airport.

"Step on it!" Alex told the driver. "We have a 10:15 flight we have to catch."

The driver seemed excited by this directive as it gave him permission to open it up. And he did. We were jammed in tightly and getting whipped around on the turns and thrown up and down on the bumps. It was quite an adventure. The driver got us there in no time. We now had to get our tickets printed and get through customs.

We were the only ones there and we were able to get through pretty quickly. We ran through the airport and saw our airplane sitting on the tarmac. We were pretty excited that we defied the odds and made the flight. Off we went to Fort Lauderdale in hopes of securing this runaway megayacht.

I was talking and planning with Alex the entire 45-minute flight. The planning continued as we got our stuff and a rental car and headed over to Pier 66 for lunch. We were tracking the yacht and knew it was still more than an hour out and was still headed towards us. We were getting excited. We had planned this heist out in great detail. We were ready.

Soon, we looked to the sea and were able to make out our yacht. We watched it approach and once it turned towards an inlet, we went to the nearest bridge and watched it pass under us. We then watched it make a right-hand turn on New River. We knew of a contact the debtor had in a house off of New River, so we went there to see if he was taking the boat there.

We hopped in our car and went into the cul-de-sac neighborhood. We saw the boat pulling in behind the house, so we parked up the street. We walked down and noticed the house next door was for sale. We couldn't legally enter a private property, so went into the neighbor's yard and leaned over the fence watching to yacht dock.

An attractive woman in a sundress got off the boat first and noticed us looking. She asked if we wanted to see the boat and invited us over. This was all I needed. Over I went and our captain and mechanic began looking the boat over. We caught the lines being tossed over and tied up the boat for them.

I asked another woman if the owner of the boat was there. She called him and he came to the railing. He refused to come down to talk in private, so I yelled up to him, for all to hear, that we had repossessed the boat and he had to leave. He had the emotional fit I expected and then went to call the bank. It turned out, the bank actually feared this man. Moments later I get a call from the bank telling me to allow them to stay on the boat overnight and to check on it. I told them this was a terrible idea, but they didn't care.

After a long night, with calls coming in from the now panicked bank, I decided to take Grady and watch the boat from the road. It was about 6:30, so we sat with our coffee and binoculars and looked for any movement. All was quiet, which was a relief. We were scheduled to take over the boat at 9 am, so we would just watch it until then. Easy.

As the clock hit 8:00, we saw the nose of the boat beginning to ease away from the dock. They were making a run for it. I called Alex and told him to drop his mechanic off at the SE 3rd Ave bridge to see if the boat came his way. I took Grady to a bridge on route 842 and I went back to Pier 66. We had every exit route covered. Alex would stay in a vehicle and begin heading in whatever direction the boat went to. This was fun for me. This was Magnum P.I. stuff, I thought.

Grady gave the first call as he saw the boat heading for the Tarpon River. This meant he was not heading in my direction, so I went to pick up Grady on the bridge. At that, the mechanic called in and told us he was heading west. Alex went to a marina where he believed a yacht of this size would go, while I picked up the mechanic. The 3 of use headed to the marina and met Alex. About 40 minutes later, we saw the yacht entering the marina area. As the pulled up to the dock, we walked out and helped them tie up again. They were shocked.

The bank allowed them to keep the boat once again. They ran again. We found their boat again. This time, however, when we walked down the dock to tie up the lines, we were met by the attractive lady in the sundress. She was storming of the boat, head down and arms flailing.

"I am done with this. You guys are messed up. How do you keep finding us? I can't take this!!" She muttered.

This was the captain's wife and she decided this cat and mouse was over. It was one of the most satisfying feelings I have had in this business. Our investigation skills were so solid, that they debtor's team began to quit. It was pretty awesome. The debtor was furious.

As if this case wasn't enough, this was really where *Airplane Repo* was born. We had been green lighted to begin filming, but the network needed some more concept information immediately. The producers would call me every 15 minutes and I was working the greatest case of my life. I couldn't just stop working to get them what they needed. The producers were eager to get one of their first shows on the air. I understood, but I couldn't drop this case for them. The continued to threaten me by saying the show will not get picked up if I didn't respond. I told them to cancel it if they needed to. Needless to say, that didn't happen.

Everything did get worked out with the network, obviously. We met with the captain and his wife later that night. We found out the captain was owed over

$100,000 in back payments and we had convinced the bank to pay the captain. As a result, he agreed to show our captain all of the quirks and nuances of this yacht. The more time our guy could get, the better for us. As we were leaving, she said something pretty incredible.

"I am glad you didn't have cameras with you. This would be a great television show."

If she only knew.

CHAPTER 9: *Cracking the Case*

One of the things that first attracted me to the repo business was the idea of doing detective work. There is nothing I like more than digging in, doing my homework, chasing leads and then putting all of the pieces together. It is very gratifying when you uncover that one piece of information that pulls the whole investigation together.

Once, I was looking for a 47-foot Fountain Lightning speed boat. The debtor lived in Little Rock, Arkansas and the bank let us know they thought this speed boat was nearby. As soon as we saw this, we knew it didn't make sense. You see, this boat had triple 550-hp motors designed for incredible speeds. It wouldn't be on any of the rivers that snake through that area.

I began to look further out and try to determine where boaters from Little Rock go on vacation and I found a couple of spots. There was Sardis Lake, which is about 90 mins southeast of Memphis. There were also smaller lakes just south of Sardis Lake, but they didn't make as much sense to us. The most obvious one was Pickwick Lake, which sits on the border of Alabama and Mississippi. It was further away than the other lakes, but was much larger and made more sense for a boat like this. I kept that in my back pocket and began doing additional research to make sure that my hunch was accurate.

While digging through the paperwork, I noticed the debtor had been racing the boat. At one point, he had a boat racing sponsor in Mississippi. Then, we looked up the sponsor's company page and found the headquarters was on Pickwick Lake. This lake is a large body of water that hosted boat races all the time. This would be my starting point

I found this info in the morning and was on a flight within two hours. While on the way, Glenda did what she does best. She picked a marina, made a call and got confirmation that my boat was there. The most difficult part of this repossession was a storm I encountered heading to the airport when I was done. Often times, when we rush out to do a repossession like this, we don't get the chance to check on things like weather. There was a nasty spring storm with tornado warnings in the area. The repo went smoothly, but the trip home that night was anything but. This was a really good case for us.

Cracking the case also requires us to talk to people and convince them to give us good information. There was a Cessna 414 twin engine airplane I was looking for on the east coast of Florida.

We had done some work and determined where we thought the airplane was. We jumped in our car and went there immediately. We were excited to have found this one so quickly and were looking forward to getting this home to our airport only to find out the airplane had left within the hour. The person at the front desk said she had no idea where they were headed. Just that they seemed like nice people.

I decided to go outside and try to talk to a line guy to get some information. I looked around for a minute or two and finally found one just walking the tarmac. I asked him about our airplane and without hesitation, he told me they were heading to the Daytona Airport. Perfect. It was a short 45-minute ride from where I was, so off I went.

When I arrived at Daytona it was after dark. The place was nearly abandoned. At first, I didn't see anyone. Finally, I found someone at the front desk willing to talk. I asked her if the plane had arrived.

She said it arrived, dropped something off and went to

a 3rd airport, which was closer to my home office. The

3rd airport was one I worked at before and I knew

people there. I got in my car and called my contacts

there. They said they were not there, but if I found

the airplane to call them back. An hour later, I arrived

at the airport. I saw a pilot there and asked him about

the plane. He told me he saw it taxiing to the back

part of the airport. I called my contact and went to the

back on my own. I walked so it took a few minutes,

but sure enough I found it and repossessed it. It

didn't take more than 15 or 20 minutes for my pilot to

get there and he locked it in his hangar at the field. A

perfect ending.

I am often surprised at the length debtors will

go in order to hold on to their assets. I don't know if

they think they get to keep it without paying for it, or if

they just believe, against all odds, that if given just a little more time, they can pull the funds together. Some have no idea that their toys can be repossessed. Some people are just hateful. They will do everything in their power to hurt anyone or anything that tries to make them pay for their toys.

We were assigned a boat in the Keys of Florida one. This was when we first had film crews for the televisions show working with us. They were doing a lot of testing of angles, shots and ways to tell the story, which made things pretty difficult for us. We had done some work on the boat in the office and had been able to eliminate some marinas and locations as potential hiding places for this one. The boat we were looking for was a 32-foot center console that they were using to fish. It was valued at somewhere in the $175,000 range, so the film crew was excited. This boat was not being used for income, just pleasure.

You wouldn't know that by the lengths these two debtors went. When we got to the house we looked around a bit and then found the boat docked in the back yard. We spent a few minutes surveying the location and then decided to make our move. It was just about 7 am and the sun was just coming up in the Keys. We had spoken to the debtors previously, so they knew we were after them. We also knew they were just bad people, so we were on guard for sure.

I went with another person to make sure we could move fast and had an extra set of eyes. That turned out to be a good move. As we approached he went ahead of me. I lagged a few steps behind and was looking at the house, property and neighborhood. I was looking for any sign of a problem. As my partner started walking down the sidewalk to the boat, I saw something glisten.

"STOP!" I yelled to him.

He did stop quickly and he looked at me with a puzzled look.

"Why?" he asked.

"There is something going across the sidewalk. It might be a spider web, but go slow and make sure." I instructed him.

As he got closer, he saw what I did. It wasn't a web at all. The debtors had used thin fishing line to create a web and placed hooks at eye level to try and hook us! We sliced the line and cautiously went about our business, knowing this could have been bad. Had we not done the research first, we would have been injured. The investigation helps in all aspects.

My favorite investigation was an asset investigation only. It was not even intended to be for a repo. A bank was ready to lend a guy

$125,000,000 and at the last second, decided to investigate the guy and make sure he was a good risk. They called me asked me to do a "quick" investigation to make sure they were good to lend the money.

They explained it was an asset based loan, so the risk was minimal. "On a $125,000,000 loan??" I thought. The borrower told the bank that he was planning on using the money to turn a closed brewery into a bottled water plant. It was supposedly the best water in the country and, the bank explained, the borrower was prepared to turn this loan into a huge business. I asked some questions about the planned operation, then asked for paperwork.

The bank sent everything over to me and, within minutes I told them to hold off. The financials showed the borrower to have a net worth of nearly $600 million. Pretty good start, right? Not so fast. I noticed he had an accounts receivable for about $590 million. The entity that owed him the money? That would be himself. I looked for the corresponding accounts payable and there was none. Almost all of his net worth was money he owed himself. I told the bank he wasn't worth much at all and if he did this on the financials, who knew what other issues there were. They told me I had one month and to proceed.

I began with some internet searches of the borrower. On page one of the search, I saw an arrest of this guy from a couple years before. Turns out, his first paying job was deceiving old people out of their money with the promise of millions in return. This information turned up the intensity on my investigation ten-fold. Over the course of the next 2 weeks, I gathered so much information on this person and his business pursuits it was almost scary. It was time to head to the field for some live investigations.

I found out he had used some of his money to purchase racehorses in Kentucky. I decided to check out the stables where the horses were kept, but knew I would stand out like a sore thumb. I started asking around as if I was interviewing them to house and manage some horses I had. I, of course, was an uber-wealthy guy, so money was no object. That is what these folks wanted to hear, so they did everything they could to impress me and win me over. They started talking and before I knew it, I had addresses, businesses and, most intriguing of all, information of his new Russian mail-order bride.

I called the bank to let them know all I had found. They asked if I had heard anything about one specific horse. I told them that was one of 22 on my list. They then asked about some of the other horses and came back to the first horse again.

"Do you know where they keep this horse?" the banker asked.

"Yes. Texas. Listen, why so many questions about this one horse?" I asked.

"Well, we actually have a loan on this horse and he is a few months behind. Do you think you could repossess him?" she said.

I was stunned for a second. I never considered repossessing a living, breathing animal. A horse can die! That was the thought that kept running through my head when I blurted out.

"Of course we can. Not a problem."

I immediately regretted my reaction to take the case. I then told the banker I would need some time to get a team together to repossess the animal. I also said there would be some unusual expenses. She said she understood and to please get him as soon as possible. I confirmed with her and hung up.

"What did I just agree to do?" I asked Glenda, who was sitting across the room.

"You do that stuff all the time. Now how are you going to get it?" she asked, very matter of factly.

I decided I would call in a guy who worked on horse farms to get this with me. I figured he had all of the knowledge that I lacked. Where was the VIN? (the number is tattooed in their upper lip.) How often do they eat? Do they get stressed easily? All of these things were running through my mind. The horse trainer reassured me he knew exactly what to do and told me not to worry. Perfect!

He then talked about all of the things he would need to pull this off. A horse trailer, food, water, a bridle...the list was extensive. I approved it all immediately. I then had to devise a plan to distract the manager so we could get this horse out.

I decided I had to go undercover and present myself as a writer for a horse racing magazine. I created a new publication called "Southwest Racing" to use for my interview. I believed the manager would know any existing publications and could check up on my validity, so went with a made up one that couldn't be found or verified.

I first had to secure the interview with a phone call. I prepped for this and made calls to my friends to make sure I sounded convincing. This was early on and I hadn't done anything like this before, so I was nervous. I knew this was my best way to get the horse repossessed, so really worked at it. What I didn't consider is how excited he might be about a magazine covering him and his company.

I checked with my partner on this case to make sure he had everything lined up. He did, so I asked for an exact date when he wanted to go. He told me that Friday was best, so I called the manager of the stables. I was very nervous. If I blew the call, I would likely blow the entire repo. I made the call and got past the receptionist to talk to the manager.

"Hello Mr. Smith. This is Ken Cage calling from Southwest Racing magazine. We are a new publication dedicated to the horse racing scene in the southwest and I was wondering if I could interview you for the magazine." I said. I pulled it off without any slips at all. Smooth.

"Sure. I would love to. That sounds great. When did you want to do it?" the manager asked. I confirmed the interview for Friday, just as we had planned. I felt more relief than pride at being able to pull this one off. The funny thing was, I was not the least bit concerned about the face to face meeting. I had been getting into places and events for years by making up personas. This was old hat. It never crossed my mind it could fail.

When Friday came, I was prepared. I was bringing a friend with a camera, who would snap some pictures. I had a list of questions and a notepad to take notes. Most importantly, my guy had everything set to repo the horse. I was calm driving over to the stable as I had planned things in great detail. I was joking with my camera guy, who had no idea how to use the equipment he was holding. We were relaxed.

I parked and started walking to the manager's office. As I was about to knock, a huge rush of adrenaline came over me. I got nervous. I stopped thinking clearly. As I tried harder to get my thoughts together, it became more difficult to do so. This was not what I expected at all. I pulled back for a second and shook my head. I was getting my bearings back. It was go time.

I knocked on the door and began "interviewing" this unknowing manager. It was going really well too. We were laughing and talking easily. He had no idea. I was keeping an eye on my phone the entire time. I told the manager this was because my office could be calling me at any time if we had any production issues and I had to take her calls. He accepted that excuse.

My guy was supposed to text me when he had the horse and was off the premises. I had a time clock in my head as to how long this should take. I got to a point where I felt it should be done, so I asked if we could get a quick tour so we could get some photos. He was thrilled at the suggestion. I would sneak off and look for the trailer while the photographer pretended to take the pictures. I saw the trailer was missing, so I quickly called my guy. He told me he was tending to the horse and forgot to text, but they were clear.

At that, I went back to the photographer and told him we had enough. I politely, but quickly, thanked the manager and walked as confidently as I could, hoping the manager wouldn't notice a horse missing. We made it to the car and offsite. We had just successfully repossessed a racehorse. The case was not concluded though.

I ultimately found that this guy was involved in an iron ore business in New Mexico. He had defrauded a business man out of seven figures in another scheme. I had literally compiled 300 pages on this guy. I submitted it to the bank and, of course, they didn't pursue the loan with this guy. We had literally saved the bank $125,000,000 they were ready to lend to this guy.

The best part of this story didn't occur for another year or so though. I was looking for a fishing boat on Lake Wylie, North Carolina. The guy was a builder from New Jersey and was living there now. After a period of time, I decided to knock on the door. When the door opened, I literally felt the color leave my face. I could not believe what I was seeing. It was the Russian mail order bride for the other crook. I lost my breath and finally just asked for the debtor. She had no idea who I was, but I sure knew who she was. Her appearance shocked me like nothing else has in this business. Fortunately, I was able to get all of the assets I needed to from her husbands. I hope every day that I never see her again.

CHAPTER 10: *A Good Partner*

I would be remiss if I didn't spend some time discussing the tv show here. While a few had seen or heard about me through the press, the vast majority of you reading this book know me from the show. The show has done some things for me that could never have happened without it. This book being one of them. I thought this chapter was a good time to step back and look at some *Airplane Repo* stories.

I first started filming for *Airplane Repo* in December of 2012. The concept was submitted and IRG was going to be one of three teams for the show. I was the only one who had cases to run though, so for the first few months, I had everyone with us. All 3 production teams were trying to learn how to shoot this kind of action and how to tell the stories. This lasted until the end of January, when we stopped filming.

I didn't know if we were done filming for good or if this was temporary. The production crew was frustrated with how difficult it was to tell the stories. They were frustrated to only have one team repossessing things. They were not sure if the people that were working with me made great partners for a show. So, we all went on a filming sabbatical. I thought this was the end. I was ok with that too. To be honest, it was much more difficult and invasive than I had imagined.

They called about a month later and said we were back on, with some changes. The production crew said they met with Discovery and had come up with a solid plan to film the show. They flew me out to Phoenix, which is where my next repo was. They put me up in a beautiful hotel near Sedona and treated me very well. I could get used to this. We were all set to film the next day.

I woke up early to prepare to get the repo done. They told me that we would head out after lunch. I thought this was a little late, but after seeing so many private and very quiet meetings without me, I accepted it. I had just 4 on my film team now, Paul Taggart, Brian Miller, Peter McCabe and Cara Freeman. Each had been working in this world for a long time and I had a lot of confidence in them. They all had great stories about their exploits. Peter spent time with Stevie Nicks and Fleetwood Mac. Brian had great stories from filming *Deadliest Catch*. It was a fun crew. We also had one of the Executive Producers with us, David Newsom. David met with Paul and Brian a lot and I just minded my business.

We all met across the street at a pub for lunch. They finished up and told me to take my time. I was doing some final preparations for the repo I was doing that day in addition to answering work emails and working on other cases. I didn't even notice when David walked in with a hulking figure with a leather jacket on.

"Ken, didn't you say you were looking for a muscle guy to work with you?" David asked as I looked up.

"Yeah. I did. Why do you ask?"

"I want you to meet a friend of mine. Danny Thompson. He has been a bail bondsman for almost 15 years and has caught over 3500 criminals. I thought you might want to meet him." David explained.

I never once wondered how David's "friend" could have caught up to us near Sedona. Like I said, I was knee deep in my company's work. The truth is, I really did need someone and he had an impressive background. I was all for filling a position while filming. We sat at the bar and exchanged small talk. The one thing that immediately impressed me about Danny, other than the obvious size of the man, was how polite he was. I got a good feeling, so asked if we could do an interview there. He agreed.

I told him I would not be asking a lot of questions, but he needed to answer completely honestly. He understood. I played this up several times and gauged his reaction each time. I had already decided I would definitely give him a shot.

"Danny, this is going to be a one question interview now. Give me your most honest answer. This is absolutely critical because, if you answer wrong or dishonestly, we cannot work together." I said with as much seriousness as I could muster.

"Yes sir. I will give you an honest answer." He responded quietly.

"OK. Completely honest. I need to know.....Carolina or Duke?" I asked, after building up the dramatic effect.

His face dropped and I could tell he was both relieved and puzzled.

"Carolina, of course." He responded.

"OK. You are in. I will be in touch shortly." I responded.

I am not sure he believed this was the extent of the interview, but it was. When you have worked as a bounty hunter for 15 years and had a track record like his, he was worth a shot. Just then David walked in.

"How did it go?" he asked excitedly.

I explained it went well and we would begin working together on the next case.

"That's great. Mic him up." David instructed

Peter. Just like that, IRG became "Ken and Danny"

on the show. I stood there trying to figure out what

happened for a minute. There wasn't much time for

that though. We immediately left to work on the

Beech Baron case that you saw in episode 1. Not 15

minutes into the case, Danny got pulled over by a

police officer. I think he rolled through a stop sign. I

asked him if he had any weapons.

"Not that I know of." He responded.

"Well do you have any warrants or anything

that could get us in trouble??" I asked in a more

panicked tone.

"Not that I am aware of."

Just then the officer comes to the door. Danny

gave me a wink and handled the officer, who just

gave him a warning. He then asked the officer for

some information about the debtor and off we went.

No weapons. No crimes. Danny got me back. At this

point, I realized we could get along just fine.

For the first season, there was a lot of feeling

each other out, as you might expect. We were getting

to know each other. We were both filming for the first

time and dealing with a crew we didn't know

particularly well, but we liked them all. I usually have

a good time with people as I get to know them. I will

joke around, maybe prank them once or twice. I like

to see how they respond. Danny takes it well and

then gives it back in a big way. Needless to say, we

had a good time.

I have told stories at speaking engagements

we have done together about some of my pranks.

Once, when we were on the floatplane in the middle

of the Everglades, Danny was napping on the float.

We had repossessed this thing at about 4 am and had

paddled the plane for a couple of hours to get away from the debtor's house. We were exhausted. I had called the pilot and he was on our fan boat heading out to us. I saw a rope dangling from the airplane on Danny's side and thought that was as good a time as any for a joke. So, I picked up the rope and tossed it softly on a sleeping Danny while yelling "SNAKE!!" Well Danny jumped up, nearly falling off the float and let me know, in no uncertain terms, that my day was coming.

Danny and I really enjoyed our time together in Season 1. I would make fun of his "Breakfast of Champions" – Danny would start every day with two honey buns and a Red Bull – and he would make fun of my dress shirts and dress shoes. It was all light fun and soon, we joined forces to have some fun with the crew. The friendship was born and it has grown over the years. Seasons 2 and 3 were so easy to make because we did have a friendship and trust that allowed us to try things in an effort to make the show better. Neither of us was worried about which one would look better or who the star was. We were fully committed to making a great show.

We have continued to work together, but only on bigger cases. Danny has his shop in Matthews, NC, TEK Automotive and he needs to continue working there. He cannot break away as often as we both would like, but he is a busy man. We did get to go to Jamaica on an extremely interesting case that nearly went horribly wrong.

This was between seasons 2 and 3 and I had a case in Miami and another in Jamaica. I asked Danny to come along and he agreed. The case in Miami was for a 40-foot boat. It was worth somewhere around $300,000. We met up in Miami and had dinner while going over the case. I had given us one day to find and secure th

day we would be on an airplane to Je

scoured the case information over dinnei.

great detail about the debtor, his company, ti.

possible locations and more. We finally wrappeo

at about 10:30 pm and called it a night.

We had to be up and on the road before 7 am

the next morning to give us the time to find and

secure the boat and we started running hard. We

checked a couple of marinas with no luck. We then

ran two addresses that we had found, but again no

luck. It was getting close to 11 am and I decided to

make a dramatic push by just going to the business

and confronting him on his turf. Danny would stand

guard and be an extra set of eyes while I went in.

The receptionist told me the debtor was not in

and wasn't expected in that day. I asked when he

was expected back and she told me she didn't know.

soon as we exited the building, Danny quickly shot out "She's lying man. I think I saw him go in the back." I also felt she was lying, so went to check on the person that went in the back. Danny told me the car he was driving and, sure enough, it was registered to the debtor. We worked our way to the back and found the debtor. Danny sat back, hands on hips staring at the debtor while I asked where the boat was. Within minutes he had given me the location and we were gone. An hour later we had it.

We celebrated in our traditional way. We grabbed a steak and a beverage and got to work on the next case. Jamaica was a place I had not been to before and I did not have any real contacts there. I was excited to add the "notch to my belt" but I was also concerned about the unknown. We studied hard that night. We were looking for a twin airplane that was being used as a transport plane. It was my belief us one day to find and secure the boat. The following day we would be on an airplane to Jamaica. We scoured the case information over dinner, going into great detail about the debtor, his company, the boat, possible locations and more. We finally wrapped up at about 10:30 pm and called it a night.

We had to be up and on the road before 7 am the next morning to give us the time to find and secure the boat and we started running hard. We checked a couple of marinas with no luck. We then ran two addresses that we had found, but again no luck. It was getting close to 11 am and I decided to make a dramatic push by just going to the business and confronting him on his turf. Danny would stand guard and be an extra set of eyes while I went in.

The receptionist told me the debtor was not in and wasn't expected in that day. I asked when he was expected back and she told me she didn't know.

As soon as we exited the building, Danny quickly shot out "She's lying man. I think I saw him go in the back." I also felt she was lying, so went to check on the person that went in the back. Danny told me the car he was driving and, sure enough, it was registered to the debtor. We worked our way to the back and found the debtor. Danny sat back, hands on hips staring at the debtor while I asked where the boat was. Within minutes he had given me the location and we were gone. An hour later we had it.

We celebrated in our traditional way. We grabbed a steak and a beverage and got to work on the next case. Jamaica was a place I had not been to before and I did not have any real contacts there. I was excited to add the "notch to my belt" but I was also concerned about the unknown. We studied hard that night. We were looking for a twin airplane that was being used as a transport plane. It was my belief that the material being transported was not necessarily legal. This was a huge topic of discussion over dinner.

We had studied as much as we could and felt confident as we boarded the airplane in Miami. We landed in Kingston and, rather than try to drive on the wrong side of the road, we picked up a cab. They drove us about 40 minutes at break neck speed to the airport where we thought the airplane was. He drove us around the perimeter and we got to see the lay of the land. I asked him to drop us off at an opening about 200 yards from the FBO office. We looked around briefly and I spotted the plane on the tarmac. Danny and I split up, as he continued checking the perimeter for an opening and I went closer to the FBO for a look.

The airport had little to no aircraft activity. It seemed as though nobody there was working on or moving any airplanes. There were two cars sitting outside of the FBO and they were both older cars. I was checking everything out when Danny walked towards me with a quick pace and real concern in his eyes.

"What's up Danny?" I asked

"Braw, I just got threatened by some guys with AR-15s" he responded while out of breath.

I checked to make sure he was unharmed and got more details. It turned out these guards were guarding the perimeter and our airplane. We were not going to sneak on to this airport. This was what I feared. I didn't know anyone at or near the airport. I had no contacts who could help us here. We were on our own so we went through the front door. I saw a woman sitting at a desk well behind the counter and tried to engage her. She never looked up as she asked what we wanted. I explained what we were there for and she told me to stay right where I was. Nothing else. A couple of minutes later, a man who turned out to be the airport manager approached me and took us into his office. We explained the situation, showed him the paperwork and then offered to pay any outstanding bills. The manager became much more helpful after that. We ended up being in the airport manager's office for about three hours then were escorted to the airplane. It turns out the debtor hadn't paid his bills for anything, so people on the island took the engines instead. This airplane was supposed to be worth $200,000+, but because it had been ripped apart, was sold for about $30,000. We didn't make nearly what we had hoped but we had a great story.

While Danny is the only partner people outside of IRG know, I have had several over the years.

Some have worked only a few cases and didn't work out and some have worked hundreds with me. I won't list names because many of the splits were not amicable. This is a very difficult business and does not always attract the highest character people working in it.

The one partner I had, worked with me on over 300 repossessions. I considered him a friend and the partnership broke up for all of the wrong reasons. We had gone on many trips together and were incredibly successful together. I took him to banks with me and he was supposed to be the person that did the show with me. When I was offered a contract in 2010, it was with him as my partner. The final straw was the television show offer in 2012. Originally, the offer was to have us as a team. The production company spoke to him on the side though and convinced him to work independently as a competitor of mine. If not for unreasonable contract demands, he might have been on the show opposite me.

In the end, getting a good partner has been a challenge for me. Everyone says they can do it, but they are fascinated by the fun stuff. The adrenaline rushes. When they have to sit in a car for 10 hours with no food, drink or bathroom breaks, they scatter. They think they will become instant millionaires, but it doesn't work that way. Finding a good partner has been the toughest part of this job for me. Luckily, I found one good one.

CHAPTER 11: *Airplane Repo is Born*

My journey to getting the television show started years before the first episode aired. People often ask me how I got on the show and I tell them a quick version, but it actually took a lot longer with a lot of twists and turns. I often start the story with *The Wall Street Journal* article. While that front-page article was absolutely a monumental step, it was not the first step. It started about a year earlier.

I had worked the week in Florida getting a couple of repos and was in the Orlando International Airport, as I had found myself dozens of times before. It was a Friday night in January, 2009 and I was heading home. This was the part of the job I loved and hated the most. The trips never went as smoothly as I wanted and today was no different. My flight to Philadelphia was delayed as the incoming flight had faced some winter weather problems getting in. I was frustrated. It was then I noticed a call coming in from an unknown local number. I hit the ignore button, as I usually do with unknown numbers.

I was shocked and, in all honesty, excited. It was a reporter for the *Orlando Sentinel* newspaper. His name was Jim Stratton and he "had a few questions" for me about the sluggish economy. I found a quiet gate, took off my winter coat and called him back. I was on the phone with Jim for about 35 minutes answering all of his questions. It turns out Jim had already interviewed a car repo guy and it seems the answers he was getting from me surprised him a bit. We were talking about $300,000 airplanes after he had been talking about $20,000 cars.

The article hit the newspapers on February 14, 2009. The economy was awful at this time and the unique thing about this collapse was how hard it was hitting the wealthy. This was something that the media found to be very interesting. It wasn't much longer, maybe two weeks, before I got a call from an international media organization called Voices Of America to do a video piece. This would be my first interview on camera. It was a straight interview piece, that was done in my office. It is funny to look back on that piece and see how stiff I was compared to now.

A few weeks later, I got one of my big breaks. I got a call from someone from the *Inside Edition* television show. They wanted to spend a day following me on a repossession and doing some interviews. This seemed like a big deal because it was an entertainment show and, sure enough, it was a big deal. I thought it was cool to have Deborah Norville talk about me before and after the story, but thought that was the extent of it. Not even close.

A day or two later I got an email from a television producer, Kevin Harris, who worked with

Mark Burnett on season 1 of *The Apprentice* starring a certain New York real estate guy. We set up a call and I learned that this producer's partner would be a man who worked for NBC television. This was serious. We had a few cases in LA the following week, so we tied the meeting into that trip. I was beyond excited. We got the address to meet and were told we would have to give our names to the lot attendant when we got there. As we pulled up we saw the giant NBC letters. We were meeting on the NBC lot. This was becoming surreal.

It was a great meeting. We all got along really well. I especially liked Kevin. He was pretty down to earth and had an excellent vision of what the show would look like. I was hooked. By the end of the meeting, I had my first television producer. It was then that I first considered that I might do a reality television show. And I was liking it.

From there, I had some regular press while filming a sizzle reel and trying to pitch the idea of a show about what I do to networks. The producers were able to get us a meeting with the Discovery network in LA at the Discovery building. We met with some of the Executive Producers there and they seemed very interested. Sure enough, they wanted to sign me to do a show. I received a contract from the network a few days later and I immediately began reviewing it. I was going to have my own show. I was excited and I was ready. We began discussing possible story ideas and I formed a friendship with the producer that was growing. All seemed good.

I was reviewing the contract and had a few questions for the network. I called my contact and she instructed me to hold off. She didn't really give me a reason or an indication that there was an issue. It turned out that another airplane repo guy was getting a look. The networks had turned him down multiple times. They didn't think he could make a good show, but he had teamed up with one of the legends of reality television, Craig Pilligian. Craig had made such monster hits such as *Survivor, Deadliest Catch* and *Orange County Choppers*. When Craig goes to a network, they open up their pocketbooks. Just that quickly, my tv show was cancelled. They were going with Craig's group.

During this time, I had heard from a reporter from *The Wall Street Journal*. His name was Robert Frank. I did some investigation and learned that Robert focused on the "high beta rich." He especially studied the dynamics of what makes that group succeed and fail. We spoke briefly during the introductory phone call and I hung up believing Robert wasn't very interested. Within a couple of days, he was asking to do a ride-along with us. I jumped at the chance.

The article did not only appear in *The Wall Street Journal*, it made the front page, just below the fold. There was a picture of a $10,000,000 jet I had recently repossessed and an ink blot picture of me. It actually took my breath away. The headline read "Cries of 'Hey, That's my Jet Don't Deter High-End Repo Men." The article was flattering and honest. I was very happy and proud and completely naïve about what was coming.

When the article hit the paper on that Monday morning in March 2010, my office phone, cell phone and emails were literally blowing up. I received dozens upon dozens of messages. Networks wanted to do ride alongs. Radio stations wanted to talk. Local, national and international media all called. By 10 am that morning, I stopped what I was doing to call my childhood best friend, Michael Forde. I told him I was losing my mind and tell me some things about the Orlando Magic, which is the organization he worked for. He laughed and gave me some reassuring words and then we just talked like old friends.

Despite all of the press, being on over 30 radio stations over the globe, on every major network and in dozens of newspapers and magazines, it still didn't translate into a show. There were many ebbs and flows. Great meetings with J-Lo's team in her office in Los Angeles and heartbreaks with networks that seemed interested. At the end of the day though, we did not have a show.

In the meantime, the show on Discovery aired 3 episodes and it did not do well at all. As the network expected, the main characters couldn't carry the action. It flopped and was abandoned by the network that fast. I am sure it was especially disappointing to know 13 episodes were ordered and only 3 aired. The thoughts of the show were pretty much dead. I believed someone else's failure would block me from having a shot.

I continued doing press as it came to me while I was doing my every day job. I would do a radio interview here or a newspaper piece there just to keep the company's name in the press, but nothing serious. I also continued to hear from television producers trying to convince me they were the company that could sell my show. In total, I heard from nearly 200 producers from around the globe. None of them were able to get a show though.

This went on until June of 2012, when I got a call while coaching my older son's baseball team in the championship series. I had been working with a producer who was a great guy and was very ethical.

We had talked about working together earlier, but nothing came of it, so when he called it was a real surprise. I was in no rush to call him back because I assumed he was just like the rest of the producers. Big on promises and small on results.

I called him the next day and he told me he had some news. I listened skeptically as he explained something that I had heard before. He had people and knew people that wanted to work with him on this project. The same old story. I politely thanked him for the call and he said "Ken, I don't think you understand what I am saying. Discovery called US and said they are ready to do the show and they want you on it." I think all of the producer talk over the years wore me out so I didn't believe this producer at first. This was the break. He told me who I should talk to and sure enough, a few months later we were filming.

The first season turned out fine, although it was quite a struggle. They pushed us very hard and didn't really respect my personal or business needs. I was also constantly pushing production to respect the fact that I owned a business that did this type of work every day. I needed to be cognizant of my business and my clients in the stories. Production wanted much more drama and excitement. If you remember, I never cut a lock or jumped a fence because that is illegal. I also never got arrested. That doesn't mean we were not getting pushed to do so.

I had filmed the first season with multiple repo partners. I had filmed approximately 5 repos that never made it to television. The format had changed a few times and I had filmed for six months, but when we were all done I was excited about what we had created. It was just a matter of waiting for the air date to see what the numbers would be. I called in some favors with some media folks to help promote the show, as the network decided they would not. I was on CNN, radio stations, Fox and a couple other places. I had done all I could to help the show.

Our first show was to air at 10 pm on a Wednesday night in July. We were all hoping for a lead in show that could generate some new viewers. Instead, they aired the old version of the show. When we heard that, we knew the viewership wouldn't be as high as it could be and it wasn't. The main thing I was concerned with was beating that show soundly and we did, despite that show being in a better time slot. The rest of the season showed some consistent, if slow, improvement despite no promotional work for the show. This was growing by word of mouth. I could also see the interest growing significantly on social media. It seemed as though we had something here.

When the final show aired for Season 1, I sat back and appreciated the opportunity and got to work on IRG work. We heard nothing from the network, so we assumed we were done. For IRG, the next several months were insanely busy and exciting. We earned and took over multiple government contracts to seize, store and sell boats and airplanes. This was a huge break for us as a company and I was satisfied that the show had helped get us some additional work and was comfortable moving on without the show.

In April, 2014 I was moving many airplanes into Houston for the contract. I was scheduling the moves, verifying them, getting to know the airport personnel and getting used to the work involved. In the middle of it all, I got a call from Danny. I skipped it and texted him I would call when I had a break. He texted back "Call ASAP. Its important." I thought there might have been a family issue, so I pulled away from the work and found an empty office to call him.

There was no furniture and I was exhausted, so I planted myself on the floor of this empty office and laid my head back on the wall. I was still hot and sweaty from being outside in the Texas heat and made the call. He told me he had spoken to the producers and Discovery a week or so before and they told him the show was picked up. He said they told him he couldn't tell anyone, including me, but he said he couldn't hold it any longer.

I was both excited and angered by this. It was great that we were getting picked up after all of this time, but could not believe they were keeping it from me. We all had contracts to work out, so I was happy they were talking with Danny. They needed to get him on board as much as me. But I have never understood why the producers would intentionally exclude me. This was a sort of precursor of what was to come.

Unfortunately, this was my experience throughout with this group. I always felt like they only had me because the network said they had to. They never appreciated the fact that I was the only one who had a repo company, a repo license, the press and was known by many all over the globe as the airplane repo guy. They wanted to create cartoon characters more than anything. It didn't help that I was constantly fighting for my company and my livelihood. So needless to say, this made the news of the pickup much more tempered. It also affected my attitude when we began planning and filming. I didn't trust many people at this point.

Season 2 was only going to be 8 episodes, instead of the normal 10. This was primarily because the production company had gone so far over budget in Season 1. This was for a variety of reasons, some controllable and some not so. They put a team together with us that I was really happy with. Gab Taraboulsy was the director and a huge baseball fan. This was a good start. Jeremy Baron had done some filming for me in Season 1 and was a nice guy and Amy Hatfield-Love was the hardest working person on the team. She was responsible for planning trips and making sure we had everything we needed. Timmy D'Antonio was also on the crew as photographer, cameraman and supported every person on the crew. He actually took the picture on the cover of this book.

The other person on the team was Jorge Abarca. Jorge was the lead camera person who had a ton of experience telling stories. He was the one that Danny and I grew closest to throughout the season. He was our confidant on the crew and the one we both trusted the most. Gab was a great guy and an incredibly talented guy, but his job was to get the story the producers wanted. That's what he was paid to do and his sole responsibility. We trusted Jorge to help us tell the story we wanted. That was key.

The show aired on Friday nights at 10 PM. Another late night, but this season we had a lead in show that we thought could help us. *Bering Sea Gold* was another gold show that had done really well following the first one and it was breaking out on its own night. The network was hopeful that they could help us get our ratings up.

The network also decided to help us by promoting the show in the media. There were tons of commercials each week to let people know about us. They also got us a ton of media. I did most of it for the show. I knew the media people and had done a lot of press before, so it made sense. I could also tell people about life as a repo man off of the show which helped. I got some dream spots too. I went to Sirius Radio and was on the *Opie with Jim Norton* show. I was a huge fan of Opie's from when he was on 94 WYSP in Philadelphia and Jim Norton is one of my favorite comedians. It was amazing. They were as hilarious as expected and far nicer. I also got to go back to Fox and appear on the *Stu Varney* show. I had met Stu when I was on Fox & Friends in 2010 and he remembered. I loved it.

My favorite spot was yet to come though. I was born and raised in Philadelphia and was a big fan of the classic rock station, 93.3 WMMR. I also had really come to enjoy the morning show team over the years. When I entered the studio area I saw pictures of all of my favorites. Geddy Lee from Rush, Bono from U2, Mick Jagger, Eddie Vedder. It was insane for me. I was greeted by some of the interns who noticed that I was a bit in awe of the surroundings. They offered me a coffee and told me to get ready.

I went on the *Preston & Steve Show* in my hometown expecting something fantastic and it was better than I thought. It was chaotic too. There were women in the studio from a local establishment. There were promoters. There was a restaurant serving food and of course, the on-air talent. I was taken aback a bit though. I was the local kid who got to be on his favorite radio show in his home town. The station that developed my love of music and I was sitting in the studio. It was surreal and the people there were the nicest I had dealt with ever.

The publicity and pairing with *Bering Sea Gold* worked. We were a top 10 show the entire season, often outperforming the show that was supposed to help us! We got as high as 2nd for the night, easily beating the 9 PM show. We were in the top 5 for nearly every episode. The network would later tell us that the lead in show disappointed in the ratings, but that made our success all the more impressive. Social media was also exploding for us. We trended most nights it was on and were a top 3 trending hashtag.

When the show's final show aired in October, 2014 I just assumed we would be picked up. We had beaten college football games, housing shows, food shows and political shows that had been on for years. I thought we could get a call before the season ended with a renewal. That never happened. In fact, the network went silent. We heard nothing good, bad or indifferent.

Time went by again and I thought for sure we were done. I had spoken to people in the UK and Australia and found out the show was huge there as well. It didn't make sense to me, but I wasn't a television expert. I was told the show was "ratings challenged" and expensive to make. Based on the negative responses, I thought that was it. Until March 2015 that is.

Five months after the show ended, I received another call. I was told we were getting renewed for a third season, but with a caveat. We would be paired with a new production company and that company would be none other than Pilgrim Films and Craig Pilligian. Yes, the same group that took the original show from me. It was meant to be. Danny and I were ecstatic. Pilgrim is the best in the business and we were convinced that the network brought them in to do several seasons. Pilgrim doesn't step into an existing show to do one season. It also gave Danny and me a fresh start with a new crew. It was perfect.

We had some phone meetings with the Executive Producer, Mike Nichols, and they got me more excited. His vision was the same as ours. He saw the same problems in the previous seasons and the opportunities he saw were in line with what Danny and I had talked about before. This was going to be our launching point.

Our team was now TEN people. We had four before, so this was shocking. Paul Baker was the director and he was awesome. He had worked on *Street Outlaws* and knew his way around a fast-paced reality show. Dan DeForest and Mitchell Long were the camera guys. They had also worked on many shows. Monroe Cummings handled the sound while Evan Ewing, Alex Cameron and Dylan Harrington assisted with all of the functions. Jenny Wilkins was the hardest working person on the team, handling every possible need in every location. The other two were usually locals that worked with us. It was staggering compared to what we were used to. It made the filming much easier and much more enjoyable.

Our team made some great episodes in Season 3. When filming was complete, we all believed we would be back together again soon working on additional episodes. We all believed we had made something pretty special, which was very satisfying. We had guys who had worked on hits such as *Wicked Tuna, Street Outlaws, Alaskan Bush People* and many more. These people knew a hit when they saw one and everyone was convinced this was a hit. We went our separate ways for the last time expecting to be reunited.

I stayed in touch with my friends at Pilgrim during the editing period, even stopping in for a visit at one point to say hello. I was doing a repo in the LA area, and surprised everyone with a visit. Mike Nichols showed me around and introduced me to the people that were working tirelessly turning 30+ hours of filming into a 13-minute story. I was amazed at the work the editors had to do. They have to sit in a dark room, looking at the tape almost frame by frame. They cut, paste, run and review tape until they have exactly what they want. It is a very challenging job and one that is critical to having a successful show. The work was moving along though and everyone at Pilgrim was as excited as I was about what the show was going to be.

As we got closer, we heard that the network hired a new person to lead it. We were told this would not affect us, but a week or so later, we found out that the network decided they would not spend one cent or one second trying to make our show – in its 3rd Season – a successful one. No commercials. No press. No articles. Nothing. They would promote new shows that failed in or after their first season.

They would promote existing shows that didn't have the viewers or support ours did. They would essentially hang us up and let us twist in the wind. No explanations were given either. It was just their decision.

This really angered me. If you are going to cheat us of our shot to be successful, at least tell us why! So, I turned that anger into energy and reached out to everyone in the media and began booking my own pieces. I went back on *The Preston & Steve Show* in my hometown. I went on Sirius and did several shows there including *The Jay Thomas Show, Freewheelin' Radio, The Sam Roberts Show and The Opie Show.* I reached out to some newspapers that did articles about the show. I was on multiple podcasts. I pushed to get the word out as best I could.

The work I was doing seemed to pay off. Over the course of 10 weeks, we were able to get more viewers per week than we did in Season 2, when they were promoting the show. Social media engagement was up dramatically. We then heard from other countries about the show's results there. I got to know a ratings person in the UK who said *Airplane Repo* was consistently "well-above benchmark" for the time slot it was being shown. Australia was seeing the same high ratings. This was all great news. But still no word from the network on renewal.

A few months had passed and the show was being shown in reruns frequently, which kept me optimistic. Danny and I were in regular contact, staying ready to start up again. We were talking to people at Pilgrim and our crew. Everyone was optimistic that a renewal was imminent. We were ready.

Sometime after the new year, I heard from someone else affiliated with the show. I assumed it was to tell me they had gotten the green light and my call was coming. It wasn't. They asked if I heard about the show. I hadn't. They told me they were called a week before by the network and told it was not being renewed. It was done. This was both shocking and disappointing. I was more furious that they would call others on the show and let them know without letting me know.

I emailed our contact from the network to tell them what I had heard. More than a week passed before I got a response. "Hi Ken, I'm sorry that the news did not come to you directly. The communication got lost in translation with all the changes at the company here. " Another sentence of small talk and that was it. I was also told I should not share the information with people publicly. Just family

and friends. This was the ultimate nail to me.
Anyone who watched or paid attention knew I put in
more time and effort than anyone. They knew I was
the only one who had a repo business to share and I
did so freely. I gave more of myself than anyone by
far. Yet the network didn't believe I was worthy of a
phone call. Think about that. I have saved the email
to this day.

I have since talked to the ratings people again
and they continue to say they were "shocked" the
show was not renewed. They said the ratings were
higher than many shows that have been renewed and
ours didn't receive any fanfare or publicity. I pointed
to a new show that stars Rob Lowe, the well-known
international movie star. Seems like an awesome guy
too. Lowe was on *The Tonight Show* promoting the
show. He had been in many entertainment
magazines promoting it. He was everywhere. He

had a **monumental** advantage over us. Yet when his show aired recently, it got about one third of our average viewership. That tends to put things in perspective.

I have begun tracking the ratings and sharing with my social media friends. I always take the averages from our Season 2 show and compare them to other shows. On most nights, we would be a top 10 show easily. Many we would be a top 5 show. On most nights we would be the highest rated show on most of the networks that would want a show like ours. The show, although called a ratings challenged show, did much better than many shows with much larger budgets and much more publicity. So why hasn't it been renewed?

At the time of this writing, there still has been nothing firm about doing another show. There were obvious flaws in the show, which could be fixed if they would allow me to do so. I mean how many times can you show the compass of an airplane and try to convince people it is the fuel gauge before you get questioned? There were so many mistakes like this and it was easy for me, the one who does this regularly, to see and shake my head.

I firmly believe the show was good and have heard from thousands of fans who are kind enough to let me know that the show was very entertaining. I am still convinced that the show, if done right, could be a monster hit. Will any network want a monster hit show? I don't know. With new players in reality television like Netflix, Apple TV, Hulu and YouTube Red, you never know. The way it ended for me didn't sit well with me. That is one of the reasons why I continue to pursue the possibility. I want it to end my way.

CHAPTER 12: *5, 4, 3, 2, 1*

You are probably reading this chapter title and thinking I am going to tell you about my rocket repo. While I did have several meetings with NASA folks about recovering things for them, it isn't about the case that almost happened. This is the story about the 5 repos I did, 4 being airplanes in 3 states, 2 time zones all in 1 day. It is one of my favorite stories. Then again, I say that a lot.

This happened during the economic crash a few years ago. I would often receive multiple assignments in one day which kept me very busy. This trip started on one of those days when the fax machine was humming. The bank had sent over 6 airplane assignments and 1 RV assignment in one day. I was excited. Several of the assets were very expensive, so I began thinking commissions. I began by doing some basic research on these airplanes and began putting a plan together. I enjoyed planning the logistics and truly loved challenging myself to repossess more assets in one day than I thought. When I left the office, I was beyond excited about the possibilities.

I decided the trip would start in Lubbock, TX. I was trying to get a nearly new Cessna 414 twin engine airplane with a $400,000 value attached to it. I flew out there and met Trever Otto, my pilot extraordinaire, for what I thought would be a fun few days. We had Duke Simily meeting us in the Dallas area for the second airplane. Duke, had gotten, not earned however, the nickname "Duke The Black Cloud" because many of the repos he went on turned out to be airplanes we couldn't fly. Duke was about 22 or 23 and he was from Staten Island. Trever, on the other hand, was from Wisconsin. Clearly the decibel level went up dramatically when Duke and I were together and Trever quietly laughed at the fun we had. We were ready to go.

Trever and I met at the airport at 6 am and got a ride across the field to the FBO. It was tight as a drum there, so we went inside and I saw a line guy who was just starting his day. I talked to him quietly and asked if he knew where the airplane was. I offered to buy his lunch for his troubles. He said he did, so off we went to the hangar. It had a lock on it. I told the guy I couldn't break into the lock, so he told me to go back to the FBO and he would call the debtor. He came back in about 20 minutes later and said the hangar was unlocked. "I talked to the owner. No questions please." I agreed and went to see the beautiful twin engine piston airplane. Trever began looking over the airplane and prepared it for flight.

We were in the air an hour or so later, headed on the short flight to meet with Duke. I was in the right seat and asking Trever many questions about the aircraft. I then heard a pilot on the headset say there was a line of really bad thunderstorms brewing just to our south. I took a look and saw a massive hammerhead cloud. Trever made a slight flight adjustment to keep us away from the storm

We landed at the next airport and met with Duke. I told Duke we were headed to Alabama next so do some flight planning and fuel up the twin. I was taking Trever and going to get an RV that was supposed to be about 10-15 minutes away. The FBO was nice enough to allow me to use the crew car and off I went to the location where the RV was supposed to be. It wasn't at the house where we were told, but there was an RV park about a mile and a half up the road. We went there and, sure enough, the RV was there. I did my work on the RV and called a transport company from the auction to pick up the unit. Once the confirmed they would be out, Trever and I headed back to the airport.

"Wow Ken. 2 repos before noon. That's pretty good." Trever said.

"Hang on to your hat my man. We aren't nearly done." I responded.

We got back to the airport and Duke had the twin fueled, staged and ready to go. We were going to fly to Tuskegee, AL in search of a war plane. The flight would be just shy of 3 hours in this airplane and, with Duke and Trever at the commands, I could relax in the back. I used the time in the back to prep a bit more for the remaining cases.

The airport we were going to had incredible historical significance. This was not lost on the three of us. When I was done prepping, I began to read about the Tuskegee Airmen and the landmark accomplishments they achieved. It was humbling. To be in the location where history has been made always affects me. This was no different. As we landed and went to the airplane, I was looking around and taking it in.

After a few minutes, we could see our airplane on the tarmac. It was Vietnam era warplane that was just sitting there unprotected. We parked next to the airplane to provide some cover. Duke went to the warplane and began checking it out while Trever and I went in the FBO. The door was open, but nobody was inside. Yes, this was a rural airport. We went back to the airplane and The Black Cloud told us, as he often did, that the airplane wouldn't fly.

We called the number for the maintenance department that was on the door and talked to the maintenance guy. We explained what had happened and asked if he would be willing to get us a ferry permit for the next week. He agreed and asked us to leave a card. I took the pictures and did the condition report and within an hour we were gone again. We had gotten 3 repos done already and it was about 4 PM.

Our next flight was to Auburn University's airport. This is the part of the story I always repeat to my niece Bronwyn, since she is a Bama graduate. She loves this part. This airport was about 15-20 miles away, so we did the quick hop to the airport. We were looking for a single engine Piper. We quickly looked on the tarmac, but didn't see it. I still wanted to get all 5 repos in one day, so I went straight inside and started asking around. The FBO manager heard me and asked me into his office.

I told him what I was looking for. He told me a bit about the debtor. A good guy on hard times. He owed the airport $1000 or so in back storage, but they had given him a break because he was such a good customer. He said he would call the debtor and see if it was ok to release it, but nothing else. I was stuck and had no choice, so sat down while he called. The manager did all of the talking and by the end of the call the debtor had agreed to come to the airport. I prepared for the worst.

When he got to the airport, he walked in and made nice with all of the employees. They clearly were all very fond of him. I was feeling like "the enemy" for sure. He walked into the office where I was sitting with the manager. I waited while the two of them talked about kids, farms and business. Finally, it was my turn. I quickly explained what I was there for and who had sent me. He shook his head knowingly and told me he expected this. I dropped my guard just a bit when he said "Let's go. I will turn it over to you." Just like that, he turned over the airplane, its keys and the logbooks.

I thanked him and told him it would still be there for another week or so. I explained we were heading up north after our meeting to get another airplane. I told him we would tell the others at the airport we bought the airplane from him to allow him to save face. He really appreciated this offer. I just reinforced the fact that he could not touch the airplane or all bets were off. He said he understood and would never do that. We did our work and locked up the airplane. That was four down and one to go.

The final airplane was in New Jersey. It was a 675-mile flight to the 2nd time zone. It was getting close to 7 PM and the guys asked for dinner. I told them we didn't have time and promised them a cheesesteak from Philly if we got the next repo done. I then did my best Nick Nolte impression from the movie *48 Hours* and tossed them each a candy bar and said "Here's your dinner."

We were all getting tired. This was a grueling trip. The excitement of getting 5 in one day had long since worn out. And now we were staring at a 3 hour plus flight, if all went well. This would get us into the New Jersey airport sometime after 10 PM, which would be after the airport closed. Even if we got there that night, there was little guarantee we could secure the airplane until the next morning anyway.

I asked Trever and Duke what they wanted to do. They both said they wanted to continue. They said it with conviction and with no hesitation. It wasn't even a question for these two. I asked if they were ok to fly for that long and they insisted they were. We were going for 5. Not because it was a record or anything, but because we were prepared to continue.

We had a backup plan in the event that the airplane had any issues, but we were moving on.

One big factor into our decision was the fact that we knew the airplane we were going to secure had flown in the last 3 days. It also had flown several times in the last two weeks. The airplane was clearly airworthy. More importantly, if we didn't get it right away, it could go on the run. Our window to safely secure this airplane was small. We had to get it as soon as possible.

We left Auburn University and began the flight up north. The airport we were headed to was about a 30-minute drive to my house, so I was refueled by the thought of possibly sleeping in my own bed. I also was getting fired up again about the possibility of completing this mega-trip. I kept thinking that getting 5 assets in 3 states in 1 day was going to make a heck of a story. I never dreamed it would make pen to paper, as it has here, but I did think about the story it would make. As we got closer, I could feel the energy surging in me.

The flight north was a really good one. The twin we started the day with was flying great and gave us the ability to keep moving quickly and comfortably. I began passing the time talking with Trever and Duke as they were flying. They tested the autopilot and it was nearly perfect. Things were going great and we could begin gearing up for the final leg of this crazy and fun day.

We were approaching the airport and I was getting myself ready. I noticed my phone was nearly dead and I didn't have a wall charger. Trever's was near dead as well and Duke's was gone. This might pose a problem, so I started trying to think of some solutions. I could see the airport so I turned off the phone to preserve the final few percentage points of power. We landed fine and began looking for the airplane.

We finally found it next to the FBO, which had a light on. We rolled up and parked next to the airplane we were looking for. It was the right one. We saw some activity near the plane, so we pulled up so we were not too obvious. I asked Trever and Duke to hang around our airplane and see if they could make some pilot small talk with anyone near the plane we were repossessing. I went inside the FBO.

I called to see if anyone was inside. I got no answer. I then quickly plugged in my computer and began charging my phone on the computer. I continued checking around the FBO to see who might be in there. I did not see anyone, so I waited another 10-15 minutes to let the phone get charged enough to call the police. I then called the repossession into the police, as I knew I could get it from here. They told me they would be right out to check my paperwork. This was a normal response from the police in New Jersey.

I went outside and talked to Trever and Duke. They had talked to the pilot for the airplane we were securing. It turned out he had just landed the plane from a night time pleasure flight and was locking things up. I wanted him to leave quickly, so he didn't run into the police. I could see that was not happening. The pilot was taking his good old time securing the books, his headsets and so on. I then made a decision to go to the entrance and meet the officer there. I told Trever and Duke to hop in the plane at the first opportunity and lock themselves in. I noticed the keys were still in the airplane, so thought we would go for it.

The officer came a few minutes after I arrived at the entrance. I explained the situation and showed him my paperwork and licenses. Everything checked out fine, but the officer did not want to leave until either the debtor left or was aware of the repossession. Repossessions are civil matters, so the police by law cannot assist, appear to assist or support a repossession. This officer wanted none of that, but he was concerned there may be something more physical or dangerous and he wanted to be sure he was there. He asked me if I wanted to wait for him to leave or confront him. I chose the confrontation.

The officer sat back at a distance and watched. He was being careful to only observe in the event he was needed for a legal issue. I approached the debtor and called him from 15 feet or so from the airplane. As he approached me, I motioned to Trever to lock himself in the debtor's former airplane. Duke went to the twin we had come in. Both pilots locked themselves in. When the debtor saw this he rushed his airplane and reacted exactly as you would expect him to. He yelled and cursed at the pilot. Banged on the door and windows of the airplane. Basically, he lost it to an extent. Trever's eyes bulged as he backed away from the door the debtor was banging on.

I followed the debtor and quickly got myself between him and the airplane. He was getting angrier. He turned all of his anger on me and gave me a two-handed shot in the shoulders as he cursed me. I saw the officer get out of the car and knew I had to do something quickly. I needed to calm him down quickly, but needed to calm myself down after he took a shot at me. I stopped dead cold, stared him down and pointed within an inch of his nose and told him clearly "Don't you EVER touch me again. I can't promise you I won't lose my temper if you do that again." I didn't yell. I never do. But I was very stern and direct and it seemed to slow him down a step.

"You are stealing my airplane! What do you expect me to do?" he responded with an almost apologetic tone.

I then explained that his airplane was over 70 days past due and we were merely taking it on behalf of the bank. His shoulders slumped somewhat. I then explained my day to him and told him we were taking the airplane immediately. I then told him what his options were and to call the bank in the morning. If he paid his bill, I would return the airplane to him. He tried bargaining with me, but when I explained I didn't have authorization to do anything else he gave up. He walked sheepishly to his car and off he went.

The police officer came over to me after the debtor left. He asked what I told the guy and seemed

happy with my approach. I told him about my day that
started in Lubbock, TX and was wrapping up here in
New Jersey. I remember he laughed a bit as I told
him and then he said "Man, you have a great job." I
smiled, shook his hand and thanked him. One more
flight and we could go home. We flew 10 minutes to
an airport closer to my house and parked both planes
there for the night.

"Let's get some sleep boys." I told the pilots.

"No way Ken. You promised cheesesteaks
and we are starving." Trever said.

We got a few steaks and headed to my house.
My wife was waiting up. She asked how it went. I
said "It went good. We got them." She went to bed
and we continued eating. Duke laughed and
remarked on my comment. "It went good? We got 5
in 1 day. That is one hell of a day." It really was. All

told, we had recovered around $800,000 worth of assets on behalf of the bank. I spent a good deal of time planning this trip and the plan actually worked. I loved the logistical planning part of the job and this made me feel like I might be pretty good at this. Yes it was a heck of a day as Duke said. I was about to blow this day out though.

CHAPTER 13: *Trying the Impossible*

A few months had passed since we did the 5 repos in one day and, as expected, it made a great story. Every time I went to visit a bank or hung out with friends at a party or bar, I told this story. It was a fun one. It had it all. I wanted more though. I truly felt I could beat that record. I also believed the time was right for it. We were in a year in which we would repossess over 350 assets. I wanted more.

It was 2009 and we were going to California for repos every month. We were heading to other states, such as Florida, Michigan and Arizona a lot as well, but California was by far our busiest state. I love California, so I never minded going. I didn't like the travel time to and from, but did love times I spent there. I had mixed a visit in to Dodger Stadium on one trip. This was a dream come true for me. I had stopped to see various other landmarks such as

Universal Studios, the Rose Bowl, USC, UCLA, Pier 39, AT&T Park and more. When I got a couple of orders in California, I started to think about other places I could see. This changed quickly when I received several more assignments in California. Some in Northern Cali and some in SoCal.

Over the course of a 4-day period, I ended up receiving 9 orders from 4 different banks in California. My competitive juices started flowing and I started thinking of the ULTIMATE mega-trip. The cases ranged from east of San Francisco down to Malibu. There were airplanes, boats and buses to repo. I kept an open mind.

I began doing my research on the cases. I was able to easily locate many of the assets while doing my office investigations. I spent an inordinate amount of time planning the logistics of this trip. I wanted to push us as hard as we could, but not push so hard that we made a mistake costing us a repo or an injury. I began to see some case that looked to be easy picks though. I couldn't ignore that. I was truly caught between not wanting to push too hard and not pushing hard enough.

I decided to run it by Glenda and my sidekick for the trip. Glenda was neutral about it but she certainly didn't see the purpose in trying to do something "epic." Glenda had often commented on how many of the guys that did or wanted to do this job wanted to do it for the glory. They wanted to swoop in, fight the debtor and ride out on the white horse. She was completely right about that. Doing the dirty work was not something these people were willing to do. Sit in a hot, smelly car for 8 hours straight doing surveillance? No thanks. She thought I was falling prey to this machismo and she was pretty clear about this.

The truth was, I wanted to make as much money as possible in as short a period as possible. That is what business is about. The other factor that I always had to consider was redemptions. If I wasted a day or two, the debtor could bring the account current, meaning we made nothing. It also gave the debtor more time to hide or damage the asset. I worked every case with that sense of urgency. Get it before it's gone. That was the thinking.

I talked to my sidekick and he was totally against the idea. He thought we would kill ourselves if we pushed that hard. I had a map of California and I highlighted the journey. I explained how the trip would go. "We would start in San Francisco, go to Livermore, then south to..." I calmly told him. We were supposed to meet our producers from NBC, so hung that carrot for him as well. We would end up in Southern California and then we could take that meeting with the NBC people, I told him. I tried to be as encouraging as possible while selling him on the idea. He still was not on board with the plan. I decided I wasn't concerned with that though. We had everything in place to get this done in one day and we were going for it.

"I understand your concern. We won't rush this trip then. We will book it for you." I told him. So, I called the producers and scheduled the meeting. I called on a Thursday and they told me to meet them on the next Tuesday. That meant our trip would be Monday. I told Glenda to book the first flight out to San Francisco Monday morning and I went over the details of the trip and headed home to Philadelphia to see my wife and kids.

The weekend was spent as it normally was. Hanging out watching my kids play sports and spending time with my wife. It was early April, so I was on a baseball field. Both of my boys had games on Saturday and my daughters came to watch them play. We were all together on a brilliant weather day. I was enjoying myself at the field, but the doubt about the trip began to creep in.

As soon as the games were over, I went to my office. I checked on the cases to make sure I had the information right. I checked on my trip to make sure I had everything booked. The flights, rental car and hotel were all booked. I looked at the trip last. That was the part that concerned me the most. We could repo the assets in time, but the driving could ruin this trip. I had done all I could do. I accepted that.

Monday morning came and I left my house at about 4:30 am to catch a 6:05 flight to SFO. It was a crisp spring morning and it was still dark out. I was completely neutral at this time, thinking only about catching my flight. My sidekick was expected to land

30 minutes before me and I asked him to go to pick up the rental car. We were working to save minutes, which could lead to saving hours. It all mattered. The flight was perfect and I landed just before 8:30 am pacific time. I remember being 30 minutes early and felt a rush about this. I texted my sidekick who said he was already on the way to the car. Perfect.

9:15 AM. We had our car and were leaving the airport, headed to Livermore to pick up a 1966 Mooney M20E. With traffic, the drive would be a little over an hour. I had learned that the airplane was not airworthy, or at least been flown in quite a while. I had used a contact to help me find a mechanic that would store the airplane and get us the ferry permit. We just had to get the airplane to his shop. He wouldn't help us get it there.

We faced typical traffic and got to the airport at about 10:30 am. We drove the perimeter and I spotted our airplane. The unique tail on the Mooney made it easier to spot. It was on the same side of the field as the mechanic, which was fortunate for us. I went in the FBO and found Shannon, our California repo agent who would stay with us for the day. California has their own repo license requirements, like Florida, and you cannot repossess in the state without one. We always called Shannon.

I then walked briskly towards the door to my airplane. I looked at the attendant and told her "I am heading out to work on an airplane. I will bring you everything you need in a few minutes." She smiled and thanked me. One big hurdle cleared.

We went to the airplane and hooked up the tow bar. We pulled it a couple hundred yards to the maintenance shop and asked for the mechanic I had spoken to earlier. He helped pull it in his shop and told us he had it from there. I gave him a credit card and a phone number and off we went. I then saw the woman at the counter and explained the situation to her. I then got her copies of the repo paperwork. 10 minutes later, we were finished. ONE DONE.

11:15 AM. The next case was a small RV that was supposed to be at the owner's home near Pleasanton. The drive was about 15-20 minutes. In my itinerary, this would be a very quick repo. I reminded the team of this to try to keep us ahead of schedule.

We pulled into the neighborhood and it was definitely a new neighborhood. The houses were nice and big with massive back yards. It was easy to forget you were in NoCal here. It felt like the Midwest. I drove and we were all looking for house numbers. When we got to within a few houses, we all saw a driveway with about 4 vehicles in it. We all said

"That's GOTTA be it." almost in unison. Sure enough, that was our debtor's house.

As we got closer, we saw the RV we were looking for was in the back, parked in. Shannon verified the VIN and we began trying to determine an escape. It didn't take long. The driveway led to the yard, not a garage. If we could get this beast started, we could back it up and drive it. We all went to the RV. Shannon was look out and my sidekick and I attempted to get into the unit. We checked the side door and it was locked. The passenger's door was also locked. I went to the driver's side and sure enough, it opened. I looked around for a set of keys and found them underneath the mat.

"Got it!" I yelled to the group. I told the sidekick to hop in and drive it to a gas station I had picked out in pre-planning. It was about two miles away and on the way to the next stop. We dropped off the RV and called the auction house. They said they would have it picked up within two hours. Perfect. TWO DONE.

12:10 PM. The next case was about 20 minutes south and was also an RV. The motorhome type RVs were great because we could just drive them and drop them off. If they didn't have keys, we could call a regular tow truck and get it moved. This allowed us to complete the cases and keep moving.

We drove down Route 680 towards the next house. There was no sense of relief, excitement or celebration. We were quiet and thinking one or two cases ahead. As we reached our exit, we focused in on the next case. The neighborhood was not as nice or exclusive as the last one, so we were preparing for potential problems. My sidekick called the tow company and got them ready in case we needed them.

As we pulled into the neighborhood, we saw smaller single-level houses built close together. All of the houses had garages too. We knew if this one was blocked in, we were in trouble. We pulled up to the house and saw the RV. It was the only vehicle in the driveway. We checked around the RV for an open door and saw they were all locked. It didn't look like we would be able to drive this one away.

My sidekick saw the neighbor in the yard, so decided to talk to her. He asked if she knew anything about the RV or where keys might be. She went from minding her business to cursing a blue streak in no time flat. She was furious we were in her neighbor's driveway, asking about her neighbor's vehicle. As she began cursing, out came two little dogs barking and yipping like crazy. They were attacking the fence like it was raw meat, trying to get at my sidekick. Just then, the woman decided to open the fence and allow the dogs to get at him. He fended the dogs off as he ran to the car.

We got in the car and I told him to call the tow company back and have them pick up the RV and take it to their lot. We waited about 10 minutes for the tow truck. Luckily, the neighbor and her miniature Cujos had gone inside. The driver got out of the truck and asked why we needed it towed. I told him I couldn't get it started. He didn't ask any other questions. He hooked up the RV and towed it. I called the auction house and scheduled them to pick it up. My sidekick had been bitten by some small dogs, but we got the repo. THREE DONE!

1:00 PM. We were slightly ahead of schedule and felt good about this. The next case was about 90 minutes south. The plan had the next 3 assets within 15 minutes of each other. We pushed it as fast as we could, trying to clear every second we could. We had no time to stop for a meal, so we went through a drive through fast food lane to get lunch and kept going. About 45 minutes into the trip, we got a call from the auction telling us the first RV was picked up and they were on the way for the 2nd. This was working out great.

We began planning the next 3 units, knowing we wouldn't have time to discuss between repos. We were getting another RV and then a boat and a car from the same debtor. Shannon was still following us and we asked him if he could split off to get the car while we got the boat. He agreed. The plan was coming together.

We had an address for the next RV. We were told it was the home address, but were excited about what we saw when we got there. It was being stored on a car lot. Now, we understood this could go terribly wrong, but also knew it had the potential of going very smoothly. We verified the VIN and then I went inside to talk to the manager. I explained the situation to him and he could not have been nicer. He was unable to contact the debtor, so knew he couldn't sell it anyway. He asked if he could get paid for two weeks storage and a wash. I thought "Here we go. It's going to be like $1000."

"How much do you want?" I asked him.

"How about $125 total." He said.

I jumped at that number. It was incredibly fair. I gave him my credit card and had this one in the books. I called the auction and asked them when they could get it. They said it would be the next morning. The manager told me that was no problem. We did our pictures and condition report and we were gone. All in just about 30 minutes. FOUR DONE.

3:00 PM. Shannon went to the home address of the next debtor and my sidekick and I went to the marina that was nearby. We had gotten confirmation that the 33' boat was there a couple of days ago. This was the one that I was most worried about.

I pulled into the marina and saw most of the boats were in dry storage. I looked around for a bit and didn't spot it. I went to find the dockmaster and see if he would help me out. I told him the boat I was looking for and it did not sit well with him. He began barking about what a low-life I was for doing this and how it hurt people like him. Just then, Shannon called. I excused myself to take it. The guy just kept yelling at my sidekick.

"What's up Shannon? Your timing isn't the best." I answered.

"The car definitely isn't at his house. What do you want me to do?" he told me.

This was the first bit of really bad news on our trip. I had to come up with an idea quickly, all while hearing the marina guy yelling.

"Try his office. It's pretty close to the home." I blurted. He agreed and that fire was temporarily put out. Now back to getting yelled at.

I tried to get to the root of his problem. So, I quietly asked him what the real problem was. He explained he was owed money and he was promised the opportunity to sell the boat. I knew I needed a place to store the boat and, assuming the debtor didn't get current on the loan, I would need help selling this from 3,000 miles away from my office. I told him I could get him paid on the money he owed. I then worked out a deal to keep the boat with him and allow him to co-broker the sale if we got to sell it. I think he was shocked.

The one thing I have learned in tight situations like this is that people just want to be heard. This guy wasn't a bad guy. He was lied to by the debtor and he was concerned about the health of his business. Beyond that, he was just a regular guy. Once I acknowledged the mess he was left with and offered to help him recoup as much of his losses as possible, he became our best friend that day. He moved the boat to a more secure rack and got us everything we needed. FIVE DONE AND THE RECORD WAS TIED.

As I was doing the condition report on the boat, Shannon called. I could hear a lot of noise in the background. I asked if he was ok and he calmly answered everything was fine. I asked what the noise was and he just blew it off as some guy in the parking lot. I asked if he found the car and he said he did and said the tow truck just arrived. They would have it hooked up in a minute, he said. This was great news. SIX DONE AND A NEW RECORD.

We met up with Shannon about 40 minutes later and I asked if he knew what the guy in the parking lot was yelling about.

"Yeah. Something about his car getting repo'd from his company parking lot."

"Wait. That was the debtor? Did he mention the boat at all?" I asked.

He had not. He was so incensed about his car, that he couldn't process much else. Shannon laughed at me for not knowing the debtor was yelling. I was distracted with my own crisis, so just heard his words and didn't think beyond that.

5:00 PM. We were now heading to the 7ᵗʰ repo of the day. This was another older airplane last known to be about 100 miles from where we repossessed the boat. This was where things could get sketchy. We would be getting to the airport when things would be much slower and much more quiet. I was concerned that this could make it more difficult to get to the airplane. We would stand out more in that environment and we were driving, so it might make it more difficult to get on the field.

We drove east and discussed the airplane. We did not plan on having a pilot here because we saw the airplane had not filed a flight plan in over a year. In all likelihood, this airplane was not flying, so we needed to get on the field, repossess it and then find someone who would work with us on the field to store and perhaps prepare the airplane for a ferry flight.

I drove, so my sidekick called the maintenance shop on the field. There was only one, so no way to avoid people that might not want to work with us. He explained we were on the way and would need a ferry permit done. The maintenance guy told my sidekick that he would be happy to help and knew the airplane. The only hitch was, the shop closed at 7PM and he wouldn't do anything without seeing us and our paperwork. This meant if we were late, we would have to stay overnight and handle the repossession in the morning.

The drive would take nearly two hours during slow traffic time. How was I going to shave time off of the drive during rush hour? This had become less about the "mega-trip" and only about getting the job done. We were both extremely tired and getting miserable. Further, we were going to an agricultural part of California. We had scoped out the area and the nicest hotel was a Motel 6. This was going to be a problem.

My sidekick was from North Carolina, so he had always implied he was a NASCAR driver by proximity. I told him I was from Philly and knew how to work traffic better than he did. I kept moving along and hit little traffic that would slow me down. It was about 6:40 and I was about 10 minutes away. He got the maintenance guy to agree to meet us at the gate and to let us in.

We got there, drove right to the airplane and saw it was in really rough shape. The mechanic came over with the tug and pulled it over to his shop. We took the pictures and did the reports in 10 minutes flat. We then handled the paperwork with the maintenance shop, shook hands and left. We were literally in and out of that airport inside of 30 minutes. SEVEN DONE. This was the easiest one yet.

7:30 PM. We were in and out of there quickly. The stress of knowing the maintenance shop was closing was thick. We all felt it. Now that we had made it and gotten the repo done quickly, we all got a rush of adrenaline. All three of us felt great. We were off to the next repo, which was about 60 miles away. We were going to pick up a King Air 200 and we had a pilot waiting there for us. We called him to let him know we were heading down and asked him to poke around and see if he could locate our airplane in the meantime.

We were excited about what we had done so far, and with the prospects of completing this trip. I hooked up my iPod and began cranking some music to keep the energy up. I, of course, had a play list full of groups like Rush, U2, Rolling Stones, Who, Led Zeppelin and the Doors. My sidekick wanted country.

We settled on Rush. OK…I was driving and it was my iPod, so maybe settle was an exaggeration.

We knew the King Air had been flying regularly and believed it was in very good shape. The plane had landed at the airport we were headed to that day and we believed it was still there. More importantly, the plane had a flight plan filed with a departure time of 6:30 AM. This was not anything that concerned us. It actually encouraged us. We believed the airplane would be fueled and prepared for the flight, which was great for us. I was hopeful it was staged on the tarmac as well.

During our drive, our pilot confirmed what we had hoped. The King Air was parked near the FBO. He was doing a walk around visual check of the airplane while we drove. This repo was coming together even before we arrived! Another reason to be excited.

When we got to the airport, we found Andrew, our pilot. He had made friends with the two folks at the desk and we had no issues getting outside to the airplane as a result. He took us to the plane and it looked to be in great shape. Andrew continued checking the airplane and I tried the keys I had been given by the bank. None of them worked in the door. I tried my spare set that I had and found a key that unlocked the door. When I climbed in I was relieved. The interior was beautiful. This airplane was going to sell for a lot.

We finished everything we had to do for the bank and Andrew said he was finished with his visual check. I gave him the bank keys and he confirmed they worked in the ignition. We shook hands and headed off for the next and FINAL repossession. EIGHT DONE.

9:15 PM. We were off for the final repo. Number nine. This was an RV and was about 50 minutes south of the airport. If we were successful, we would have another drive of just over 3 hours to a waiting hotel. The drive promised to be an easy one. It was all highway until our exit, then one mile to where the RV was supposed to be.

We hadn't eaten for most of the day, so we decided we would stop on the way. We found that we had waited too long. We were now in a part of the state that shut down at 9 PM. There were no restaurants, shops or stores open. We tried well-known chains and mom and pop places. All closed by 9. We weren't going to eat. This, of course didn't sit well with Shannon and my sidekick. I promised food after the next repo and they had no choice but to agree.

We got to the given address at about 10 PM. The only problem is, the address was a UPS store. Which means a PO Box. We pulled into the lot and there were only faint street lights on. No cars. Nothing open. This was a dead end. I parked the car and tried to do some additional investigations on my phone, which never went great. I found a work address within a couple of miles, so we went there.

We got there and saw a huge warehouse. We knew the RV could be stored in there without any issue and began believing that was the likely location of the RV. We would have to wait until the next morning to confront someone there and hope they would turn it over. We would also have to cancel our morning meeting in Burbank.

I told the guys to hold tight for a minute. I looked over the report again on my phone and came across the ex-wife. That address was back near the

UPS store. "BOOM!" I said. "That thing is at her house." I boasted. And I believed it too. I turned the car around and raced to the address,

The house was in a quiet, older neighborhood. The houses were close together, but not on top of each other. It was about 10:30 now and all of the house lights were off here. It was dark and extremely quiet. There were trees in the yards and lining the streets. We turned off the radio to make sure we didn't bring any more attention to ourselves than we wanted. We crept down the street until we got the right house. I shut the car down and took a look in the driveway. I could see what looked like our RV under the tree in the drive.

We got out and walked up to the RV. As we got to about 10 feet of the vehicle, we heard dogs barking from inside the house. The house lights went on and then the porch light flashed on. The front door flung open and an older woman in a robe came out screaming at us.

"What are you doing here? Get out of my yard. I have a gun and I will use it." That was the edited version of what she yelled.

I stepped forward and verified her name. She confirmed it. I asked to approach her and explain why we were there. At this point, I noticed the neighbor's light was on as well and he was standing on the porch. She said I could approach but told me to stay about 5 feet away from the steps to the porch. I agreed. I then went through my talk about why I was there and what I wanted to do.

"That ain't mine." She instructed me. "That belongs to that jerk I used to be married to. He loves that thing."

Divorces often provide great opportunities to repossess things easily. This was no exception. She told me I could take it. She didn't care. I asked if she knew where the keys were and she told me she did, in no uncertain terms. A minute or two later she threw them to me. She told me to keep it down though. "It's a quiet neighborhood and my neighbors work in the morning. Don't be waking them up." I found this to be a funny thing for her to say. I thought "YOU are the only one making a lot of noise and you already woke your neighbors up." But this wasn't the time to argue that point.

My sidekick got into the RV and it cranked up. I was worried about that. I told him I would meet him around the corner at the gas station and we could fuel it up. I then went to Shannon and thanked him for hanging with us.

"Heck of a day, huh?" I said to Shannon.

"I thought you were nuts. I actually blocked out all day tomorrow to do these jobs. Now I have a day off." He told me.

I followed to RV as we got gas and then went 15 miles down the road to an RV storage facility. We locked it up and left a message with the auction house to pick it up. We were done. NINE IN ONE DAY! As difficult as I thought this would be, it was far worse.

It was now about 11:30 and we were staring at a 3 hour drive to our hotel. To make matter worse, we were both starving. We started on Route 99 towards Burbank. I promised to stop at the first place we found. It wasn't until about an hour and a half later that we saw a Denny's in Bakersfield. It was about 1 AM and the crowd was sketchy at best. We didn't care though. We ordered two meals each and a lot of coffee.

We ended up pulling into the hotel at 4:00 AM. Our 10 AM meeting was 10 minutes away, so we both went up to grab our couple of hours of sleep. I crashed quickly and hard. Before my head hit the pillow though, I did take a minute to think about what we had accomplished. Nine repos in one day is pretty special. These aren't cars that are all within 30 minutes of each other. These were spread out and required a lot of driving and planning. Total value of the assets this day was about $1,500,000 so it was a profitable day too.

I would never try to convince anyone that these were all difficult cases. I know many of them were pretty easy. Largely because we planned them out. My sidekick did get bit by a dog and someone threatened to shoot us, so it wasn't all easy either. The tough part was the logistical part though. If we took the cases in the wrong order, we would never have been able to do this. Any bumps would have ended the trip as well. This went as perfectly as it could have. I went to sleep with that thought.

The next day, we went to the producers and told them the story. They were wide-eyed, mouths open and smiling as we told it. "THIS is a TV show." One of them said. They told us their plan of how they would sell the show. We ate it up. We left the meeting excited about our prospects. When I got to the car, I noticed something on the ground. Someone had dropped their driver's license on the ground. As fate would have it, the license belonged to one of the producers. We went back up to their office and I slammed it on his desk. "THIS is why we should have a show. We find everything." Before they could respond, we left. It was the perfect end of the perfect day.

CHAPTER 14: *The Things I Will Never Forget*

When you do this job long enough, you forget a lot. Throughout the writing of this book, I have referred to people that know these stories to help me remember exactly how these stories went. I have done so many repos and handled so many cases, the details sometimes get lost. Some of the stories, the details or the fun stuff we experienced during the trips has been forgotten.

When I started writing this book, which took about four years of coaxing to write, I reached out to Trever and Duke. They had done the most repos with me and a lot of the crazy ones. I had some of the stories ready to go, until they started talking and telling stories I had long since forgotten. Once they started telling these stories, the details came back as fresh as ever, but without their coaxing I would have forgotten them.

There are some stories, however, which I will never forget. There are different reasons why I remember these stories. Some are gut-wrenching. Some were scary. Some were hilarious. Whatever the reason, these are some of the stories and events that I will always remember.

The first one is probably the most haunting story I remember on a repo. I was back in Northern California working on an old, beat up Cessna 337. This is a neat airplane because it has props in the front and the back of the airplane. It is unique for sure. I was able to find the airplane in a hangar at the airport. The hangar was open, so we got the airplane and locked it up. I then went looking for the logbooks.

I went to the debtor's business. Now that we had the airplane secured, he couldn't get it back so I thought I might as well go straight to him for the books. I asked the woman at the front desk if he was in. She was a younger girl, maybe 19 or 20. Her face sank and a really strange feeling came over me. She seemed very afraid of him. She told me he wasn't in. I asked for his phone number, return time and location, but she shut me down cold. I will never forget how strange that felt.

I proceeded to look for him and the logbooks. I went to his home to try to find him there. The house and yard looked unorganized. Toys out front, a swing set and a random box trailer in the yard. I knocked on the door and got no response. I then began looking around the unfenced yard for any clues about where this guy could be. As I got closer to the box trailer, I began to get goosebumps. Everything felt wrong when I got closer. I couldn't figure out what it was. As I went to investigate, I started hearing some noise from inside the trailer. When I opened the door, which was sealed shut, I was completely shocked. There were four children in there, ranging in age from about 2 to about 9. Young kids. HIS young kids were in there. No bathroom. No lights. No food. I was horrified.

I immediately called the police and asked them to respond. The youngest came to the edge of the trailer, as if to jump out. I made sure she didn't. I asked the oldest one if they were ok. She said they were. I asked why they were in there, hoping to find out they were just playing, though I knew that wasn't it.

"Daddy puts us in here after school until he gets home from work." She told me.

When I asked how late Daddy worked, she said until after dark. I told them to stay in there, but I would leave the door open. I went to the car and only a minute or two later, the police came to rescue the kids. I don't know what happened after this. My hope is these kids were cared for properly. This is still the one case that stands out for obvious reasons.

On a much lighter note, the most memorable flight was with Tom Huntington, who was with me on the NFL player's case. Tom was a surfer or skim boarder who loved the beach. He had a very mellow and laid-back attitude about him. Another thing I learned about Tom was he could sleep anywhere at any time. On this trip, we needed to repo and transport an old Mooney from Hayward, CA to Florida. I would get dropped off at the next case in Las Vegas and Tom would continue on in the Mooney.

It was a gorgeous morning in Hayward. We had repossessed and secured the airplane the night before, so when we got to the airport at 8 AM, we could just go. The airplane was fueled and staged for us when we arrived. Tom picked up some sectionals for the trip and we were off.

We started heading east towards the mountains. Once we leveled off, Tom began looking at the mountains to determine a safe place to pass. The airplane was limited on its altitude, so Tom was looking for a place in the mountain that was a bit lower. The flight to the mountains was perfect. Everything was still and you could see for miles. The views were spectacular and I was enjoying every second of the flight.

We easily cleared the mountain and were on the eastern side of the mountain. Within seconds, everything changed. The winds were whipping on this side and we were in a little, single-engine airplane. We were getting tossed around like dandelion in the wind. Tom thought this was great. I hated it. The worst for me is when the airplane would get blown up 300 feet or more by the wind. How does this make sense?

We continued on into Nevada and over the desert. At one point, Tom opened up a sectional map and began reading it. The airplane got thrown into the air and onto its right side. I was leaning heavily on the door and looking straight down. Tom didn't notice. I was holding on for what felt like minutes.

"Hey Tom. Any chance you could straighten this out?" I calmly asked Tom.

He put the sectional down and says. "Oh. Didn't even realize." Then he calmly straightened the plane out and went back to his sectional. It didn't faze him in the least. The next bit of the trip was more of the same. Winds blowing us up, then to the right, then up again and so on. It was a struggle for sure. I then heard some squawking over my headset. The only word I could make out was Thunderbird.

"What is that? What are they saying?" I asked Tom.

"Nothing. Just the Thunderbirds are practicing around us." He responded.

This was not the news I was looking for and this certainly ranked higher than "Nothing". That meant these jets were flying over the desert at about 600 mph working on maneuvers. We were going about 130 mph. The rest of this flight lasted maybe 30 minutes, but it got no better. Of all the airplanes I had flown in and all the places I have flown, this was the worst flight I had ever been on. I still remember how bad it was and how little it bothered Tom.

One of my favorite stories happened early on. It wasn't enough to warrant a chapter here, but wanted to mention it here. I had just gotten back to the office after a repo and saw two men in there talking to Glenda. One I had met before. He was a pilot from the UK and a friend of the previous owner. The other was a kid pilot I never met. Glenda told me we had a new case in Stuart, FL for an old Piper Warrior. Upon hearing this, the two pilots offered to fly me down to get it that night if I wanted. I accepted.

The kid pilot told me to hop in his Grumman so we could fly to Daytona, where he was going to school at Embry-Riddle, and we would all go down in the other pilot's Cherokee. I did and about half way into the flight, I realized I didn't even know this kid's name. Through the headset I introduced myself. He said "Oh, sorry. My name is Trever Otto." Yes, this was the first case I was going on with Trever. Neither one of us had any idea how much we would do together in the future.

We got down to Stuart at 9 PM, which was after closing. We were able to get onto the field because we flew. We pulled up right next to the Warrior we were looking for. It was in terrible shape. We quickly determined this airplane would be going nowhere fast. As I exited the airplane, I noticed a security guard patrolling. He noticed us, but didn't say anything. We were good.

We were looking over the plane and preparing the report for the bank and enjoying a nice Florida night. I called the repossession into the local police department and began taking pictures. I then noticed several sirens in the distance.

"Wow, I wonder what's going on. That's a lot of sirens." I said.

They were getting closer to us, but I didn't pay attention to it. A minute or two later, we could tell they were right around the corner. We wondered what all the fuss was about. Were we in some kind of danger? I moved away from the plane and began looking for smoke or some other clue as to what they were responding to.

They kept getting closer and then I saw the guard open the gate. Here they came. Car after car. The officers in the lead cars opened their doors and pulled their weapons, just like you see on television. They then screamed AT ME. "Put your hands up and move away from the airplane." Of course, I complied.

Two officers approached me, pistols pointing at me. They asked what I was doing there and I told them. I told them I had called it into their department about 15 minutes before. They asked who I was with. I started to tell them I was with the pilots, but when I turned to point to them, they were gone. VANISHED! My two pilots ditched me. So, I said I was there alone.

They quizzed, searched and prodded me for a bit. I kept asking them to call their dispatcher who could clear this up. Eventually someone did verify the repossession and things calmed down. I counted the police cars and officers that had responded. There were 13 cars and 20 officers. All pointing their guns at me at one point.

"Did you really need 20 officers for this?" I asked.

"There were 6 more on the way, but they got caught behind the train." The officer said laughing.

Every time I tell that story to someone who knows Stuart, they laugh and know exactly what I am talking about. They tell me it is just a Stuart thing.

Another one of my favorite cases was in Fort Lauderdale. I was with my regular sidekick at the time and we were working several cases in South Florida. On this night, we were looking for a Gulfstream G3. We had been tracking the airplane and know it had been to South America and Central America several times recently. This made us believe the airplane was doing some things they shouldn't be doing.

We had been down there enough that we had built some solid relationships. We called our contact on the field and he told us to come by after 9 PM. We went to get something to eat at Outback and then went to claim our prize. When we got there, we met our guy. He confirmed the airplane was there. The plane was being managed by some really bad guys in the back of the field. They had a hangar and nobody knew what they did back there. We had an idea.

Our contact took us to the back 40 on a tug and had us verify the airplane. That was the one. He said the guys left the airplane at about 9 every night, which is why he wanted us to wait. Made perfect sense. We hooked up to the airplane and tugged it to be staged next to the FBO. We fueled it up and told the pilot to meet us at 7. We would fly it to Orlando in the morning. I then called the repossession into the police and went to the hotel for the night.

The next morning was a perfect morning. Perfectly sunny, cool with a very slight breeze. We got to the airport before 7 am and went to get in the airplane. My sidekick was excellent at picking locks, so he tried to open the door. No luck. He went to his car to get the rest of his set. I looked at the door and tried to just open the door. The door opened right up. It was unlocked and my sidekick was trying to lock it. I stood on the top step and, as soon as he realized I had gotten the door I screamed "I GOT IT! I am a better lock-picker than you!!!" He asked how I got it and I told him it was never locked. That became a joke for quite a while.

The pilot showed up at 7:30 as scheduled and he began looking the airplane over. All seemed to be going smoothly. A few minutes later, someone from the FBO came over to the plane and asked who was in charge. I said I was. I assumed they had a bill of some sort. He then told me I had a phone call. This could have been Glenda or the debtor, so I got prepared for the worst.

I answered the phone and heard something I wasn't prepared for. It was someone from a law enforcement agency. They had heard we had repossessed the airplane and they wanted to check the airplane from nose to tail. I wasn't going to say no. He told me to go get breakfast and he would call me when he was done. By the time I told the pilot to clear the area, several people had already shown up to inspect the airplane and surrounded the area. The dogs are bigger than you would think. Lets leave it there.

I could go on and on. The Bell 206 in San Diego. The ex-wife who gave me her ex-husbands boat parked behind her house, along with his fishing gear, pictures and more. Truly, when you have done 2,000+ repos and seizures the stories are plentiful. I could easily do another book. I will finish with this story though. It is the most impactful story I have.

I was in West Florida looking for a 22-foot boat. It was a small payday, but for a big client so I worked it hard. I found out the owners were a young couple who worked for a home improvement company. It seemed the collapsing economy was swallowing them. I wanted to get this boat before they sold it or did something else with it.

I did all of my research and ran a ton of marinas and dry storage areas. Nobody knew the boat or the debtors. That didn't surprise me as this was a boating haven and the boat was a small one. I usually get to a point where I get bored with looking, so I go to confront the owners. This was where I was on this case. I decided to go to the home.

As I pulled up to the house, I noticed a Michigan State bumper sticker on the car in the driveway. That stood out for two reasons. One, you don't see a lot of MSU stickers in Western Florida. Two, I worked at Chrysler a year or so before and knew a ton of people that went there. I would use this to disarm the debtor. I knocked on the door, but there was no answer. I decided to go around back.

I went back yelling "HELLO" to make sure I didn't startle anyone. I saw some young child's toys in the backyard as I approached. Finally, a woman of about 35 got up from her chaise lounge where she had been sunbathing. I was still outside the fence as she acknowledged me. I asked if I could enter the yard to talk and she said I could.

"Hello Maam. I am Ken Cage with IRG and I have been hired to repossess your boat. I want you to tell me where it is."

She took it like it was something she expected. "Ok. Sure. It's at the marina in slip B-22" she told me. I was shocked. I asked if she had any personal property in there she wanted and she told me they cleared out the boat months ago. Since they couldn't afford it, they weren't using it.

She then began telling me her story. She and her husband bought some properties and were flipping them for a profit. They committed to only owning a maximum of three at any time. Before they knew it, property prices were declining and they had 15 properties. She said they bought one property for $250,000 and were offered $800,000 for it 3 months later. They turned it down because they wanted to build there. She said immediately after that, housing prices collapsed and they were stuck with the properties. They couldn't get rid of them at all.

"Wow. That's terrible. I'm really sorry." I responded. And I meant it.

"What are you sorry for? You didn't do anything. This is all our fault." She responded.

I explained I was sorry that happened to them. That was a tough break. She then showed so much toughness and resilience I was inspired by her. She told me what their plan was to recover. She had a step by step plan. She told me how long it would take her. She had it all figured out and had such confidence in the plan. No arrogance, just confidence. She was very impressive and she made me feel a lot better about what I was doing. People frequently try to disparage the work I do. They try to say I prey on people who are down on their luck. This woman put things in perspective.

One thing I learned early on was the cases and the money will come and go. The one thing that will remain is the stories. When I was discussing this book with Trever, he told me these were some of the best times in his life. That is pretty profound. We had a lot of fun over the years. I have been to many great places. I have had great meals, stayed in great hotels and flown in great airplanes. Most of all, I have met thousands upon thousands of great people. There are so many great stories and memories from this job. I am truly blessed.

I took my shot and went on my own. I am fortunate to have had an excellent business partner in Bob Weeks and a great office manager in Glenda. I have been lucky to make a career out of something I enjoy doing. The television show and the press I have received have all been fun. I have enjoyed seeing different places and worlds. It has been and continues to be a blast I am beyond thankful that people took an interest in what I have done and made a fun trip and amazing one!

Made in the USA
San Bernardino, CA
01 November 2017